Maths 5–11

Focusing on good progression from Reception to Year 6, *Maths 5–11* provides a clear and concise presentation of the fundamental knowledge that all primary mathematics teachers need. It provides readers with practical knowledge for the planning and assessment necessary to employ the theories expressed in the book.

Ranging from number sense and place value to looking in depth at the various aspects of fractions and mathematical reasoning, this book explores:

■ mathematical connections inside and outside of the curriculum;

■ the relation of mathematics to other primary subjects such as science, geography, and art;

■ mathematics teaching practices from high-performing jurisdictions across the world;

■ the progression of learning from primary school to secondary school;

■ the 'big ideas' in mathematics; and

■ activities that provide strategies for children to use responsively and creatively.

Helping primary teachers and mathematics coordinators improve and enhance their mathematical subject knowledge and pedagogy, *Maths 5–11* will re-instil an excitement about teaching mathematics among its readers.

Caroline Clissold is a consultant for Rising Stars, Numicon, and Inspire and was a former assistant director of National Centre for Excellence in the Teaching of Mathematics. She also has 20 years' experience as an independent mathematics consultant following many years as a primary school teacher.

The *5–11* series combines academic rigor with practical classroom experience in a tried and tested approach which has proved indispensible to both trainee PGCE students and to practicing teachers. Bringing the best and latest research knowledge to core subject areas, this series addresses the key issues surrounding the teaching of these subjects in the primary curriculum. The series aims to stay up to date by reflecting changes in government policy and is closely related to the changing curriculum for the primary core subjects.

Each book contains lesson planning guidance and methods to develop pupils' understanding as well as offering creative and innovative ways to teach subjects in the primary classroom.

Titles in this series include

Physical Education 5–11, Jonathan Doherty and Peter Brennan

History 5–11, Hilary Cooper

Modern Foreign Languages 5–11, Jane Jones and Simon Coffey

English 5–11, David Waugh and Wendy Jolliffe

Science 5–11, Alan Howe, Chris Collier, Dan Davies, Kendra McMahon & Sarah Earle

Maths 5–11, Caroline Clissold

Maths 5–11

A Guide for Teachers

Caroline Clissold

Routledge
Taylor & Francis Group

LONDON AND NEW YORK

First published 2020
by Routledge
2 Park Square, Milton Park, Abingdon, Oxon, OX14 4RN

and by Routledge
52 Vanderbilt Avenue, New York, NY 10017

Routledge is an imprint of the Taylor & Francis Group, an informa business

British Library Cataloguing-in-Publication Data
A catalogue record for this book is available from the British Library

Library of Congress Cataloging-in-Publication Data
A catalog record for this book has been requested

ISBN: 978-0-367-21967-3 (hbk)
ISBN: 978-0-367-21968-0 (pbk)
ISBN: 978-0-429-26907-3 (ebk)

Typeset in Bembo and Helvetica Neue
by Apex CoVantage, LLC

Contents

Acknowledgements

This book is dedicated to Christ Church Primary School, Hastings; Georgian Gardens Primary School, Worthing; and other schools that have the belief that what I advocate makes sense and are trying the ideas I suggest, either as part of or as a whole-school programme.

It is also dedicated to Christina Wood, who was kind enough to read the draft of this book, spotting errors and making suggestions about important things to add that I had missed.

Introduction

Welcome to the first edition of *Maths 5–11: A guide for teachers*. Over the years, many books have been published to help teachers improve and enhance their mathematical subject knowledge, their pedagogy and the various facets of teaching mathematics, including planning and assessment. This book is slightly different. There is, of course, a focus on subject knowledge and pedagogy, but there is also an emphasis on the progressions within the mathematical concepts we teach and on making connections across these mathematical concepts.

The national curriculum for mathematics was published in 2013. Most schools in England have now implemented it. Since this curriculum was introduced, several schemes of work for mathematics and mathematics books with teacher guidance and activities for children to work on have been published. Most of these rigidly follow the requirements of the national curriculum and teach them in the order that they appear.

If we are to teach mathematics successfully in primary school, we need to be mindful of the paragraph that has been written and positioned underneath the aims of the national curriculum:

> Mathematics is an interconnected subject in which pupils need to be able to move fluently between representations of mathematical ideas. The programmes of study are, by necessity, organised into apparently distinct domains, but pupils should make rich connections across mathematical ideas to develop fluency, mathematical reasoning and competence in solving increasingly sophisticated problems. They should also apply their mathematical knowledge to science and other subjects.
> (https://assets.publishing.service.gov.uk/government/uploads/ system/uploads/attachment_data/file/335158/PRIMARY_ national_curriculum_-_Mathematics_220714.pdf, 2013)

From my experience working with teachers in primary schools, connections are rarely being made, and concepts in mathematics are being taught discretely. For example, in Year 3, children look at tenths in fractions. This concept is actually part of place value, and for a depth of understanding, children need to encounter this concept within that context as well as within fractions. By using appropriate visualisations and manipulatives, particularly place-value charts, digit cards and Dienes, as well as practical measurement tasks, these two concepts link together well. As part of variation (something that we must include in our teaching and considered throughout this book), practice activities could apply this concept to measuring in centimetres and millimetres. One millimetre is one tenth of a centimetre, so linking these units of measurement to place value will help students make connections between the two concepts.

For example, I recently worked with a Year 3 class on a series of lessons about place value. Once they had understood the basics of positional, multiplicative, additive and base 10 (Ross 1989), the children were able to understand that, for example, 4.6 was 4 ones and 6 tenths and make the link to the decimal representation of 4.6. Of course, they were making these numbers using digit cards in their place-value grids and representing them with Dienes. They had all seen decimal numbers outside of school and could quote places where they had seen them, for example, at a petrol station on the sign showing the price per litre, the milometer and temperature gauges in a car! We can constantly be surprised about what children know from their home experiences, and we need to capitalise on that!

The children went on to record different numbers as tenths and decimals, recording, for example, $15\frac{7}{10} = 15.7$. We then went on to link this to measurement. As previously mentioned, an obvious link to tenths is centimetres and millimetres. We used rulers to find out how many millimetres are equivalent to one, two, three and one-and-a-half centimetres and so on. We spent some time practising drawing and measuring lines accurately. Sadly, this skill appears to not always be given enough focus in Key Stage 1, because some children had little idea about how to use a ruler other than for underlining dates, learning intentions and drawing margins! They were given strips of paper to measure and record using tenth and decimal notation. By the end of this lesson, most children were able to record, for example, 8 cm 3 mm as 8.3 cm and 83 mm. They continued practising this skill by drawing their own lines, measuring and recording in the same way. At a later date, we revisited this within a unit of work on addition and subtraction. Naturally, we dealt with whole numbers first in a series of lessons developing mental calculation strategies. We went on to practise this using the context of measurement. The children remembered the links they had made within the place value work well, finding differences and totals between measurements such as 3.5 cm and 2.3 cm by using the mental calculation strategy of sequencing (3.5 cm + 2 cm + 0.3 cm and 3.5 cm − 2 cm − 0.3 cm). Having a decimal point in the numbers did not faze them; they could see that the process of addition and subtraction was the same for numbers with decimal places as it was for whole numbers. They also understood that the process was the same no matter what units were used.

This was very successful. Both the class teacher and I were delighted by the response – and surprised. We should not have been surprised; children making connections such as these makes perfect sense! You can read more about this in the Place Value section.

As a result of working in different schools, I decided to write alternative plans which link concepts with measurement and statistics. Some schools were keen to use them; others were happy with what they were already using. A number of the interested schools have been trialing the plans and I have been carrying school-based research over the last year with some of these schools. The impact has been very positive.

One immediate impact was related to me from a Year 1 teacher whose daughter, in Year 4, was struggling with mathematics because different concepts were covered too quickly and she was not given the chance to really understand what was going on. This teacher said,

> My daughter has grown in confidence and understanding of maths. Her maths skills are being further embedded by exposure to the fundamentals of number in lots of different contexts. She says that she now "gets it" because they are doing the same thing in lots of different ways.

Hopefully, this book will help current and prospective primary school educators work with the national curriculum and consider how these links can be effectively made to give children a deeper understanding of the subject and its relevance to real life.

From my research, I have found little that links numerical concepts to measurement and statistics. To me, these are obvious links and quite simple to implement.

SecondaryMathsNatStrats authored a piece of work in June 2011 which was updated in December 2011. This work gave planning guidance for teachers of mathematics in secondary schools, showing the links between the different strands of mathematics, and suggested that these elements were an interconnected set of ideas. The organisation suggested that good planning ensured that mathematical ideas are presented in an interrelated way, not in isolation: 'Awareness of the connections helps pupils to make sense of the subject, avoid misconceptions, and retain what they learn.' It suggested presenting each topic as a whole rather than as a fragmented set of small steps. It encouraged teachers to bring together related ideas, for example, teaching measurement within the topic of place value. They talked about mathematics being a unified subject. We need to think this way as primary school teachers of mathematics.

The National Centre for Excellence in the Teaching of Mathematics (NCETM; 2018; https://www.ncetm.org.uk/) has produced a helpful visual representation on teaching for mastery. You can find it on its website.

Basically, the NCETM says that four key interconnected elements make teaching for mastery achievable. These are

- representation and structure;
- mathematical thinking;
- variation;
- fluency.

These four elements are broken down to indicate what is involved in each:

- Representation and structure involve access for all, pattern and making connections.
- Mathematical thinking involves chains of reasoning and making connections.
- Variation involves procedural variation, conceptual variation and making connections.
- Fluency involves number facts, multiplication facts and making connections.

These elements should be interconnected and revisited frequently in whatever mathematics we teach. Elements of all four must be in everything. As outlined earlier, within these are various elements specific to each. However, there is one element that is there throughout – making connections.

Making connections is a theme that appears time and again whenever we read about the effective teaching of mathematics. There is research that helps us make connections between the different number aspects of mathematics. For example, there has been recent discussion about the 'big ideas' of mathematics, which is nothing new and can be dated to Jerome Bruner and possibly before him. It has been suggested that these big ideas, particularly in number sense, are the key to developing teachers' mathematical subject knowledge, enabling them to respond more effectively to the demands of the national curriculum. Charles (2005, p. 10) defines a big idea as a statement of an idea that is central to the learning of mathematics and one that links to many other areas of understanding to create a whole piece of understanding. He contends that these connections are important because they enable children to see mathematics as a set of ideas that 'encourage a deep understanding of mathematics, enhance transfer, promote memory and reduce the amount to be remembered' (Charles 2005, p. 10).

In developing the big ideas of number sense, Chris Hurst and Derek Hurrell (2014) have suggested that the big ideas are counting, place value, multiplicative thinking, multiplicative partitioning, proportional reasoning and generalising algebraic reasoning. The first four are considered to be in the primary domain and the last two in the secondary domain. It could be argued that the last two – proportional reasoning and generalising algebraic reasoning – actually start in the primary phase of education.

You can find out more about the first big idea, trusting the count, in *Assessment for Common Misunderstandings – Introducing the Big Ideas 1* (2006) by Professor Dianne Siemon of RMIT University.

We have learned a great deal over the last few years about good practice in higher-performing jurisdictions around the world. I think it is time to take their good practices and embed them into an English approach to mastering mathematics. This includes making connections between measurement and statistics and the number-based topics. We need to do this because our curriculum is very heavy in content, and somehow, we need to make the links to reduce cognitive load for children and to cover everything that is specified in the curriculum. I also believe that we need to rearrange some of the national curriculum requirements so that concepts flow more effectively throughout the year groups. The national curriculum specifies that the requirements we have must be taught in primary school, but there is flexibility to move requirements into different year groups if we see the need. I have suggested ways to do this in various parts of this book.

My belief is that we should also re-introduce the mental calculation strategies brought to us many years ago by the National Numeracy Strategy. Mental calculation strategies were introduced into our teaching in 1999 when we followed this strategy. Since the introduction of the national curriculum, mental calculation strategies are rarely being taught. The focus tends to be on procedures for the four operations. Re-introducing these strategies so that children do not use a written column method as their default method for every calculation is important. Children should be able to reason when the written column method is appropriate and when a mental calculation strategy is quicker and more efficient. Children in Key Stage 1 do not need to learn about written column methods, so this is an ideal time to begin developing mental calculation strategies which they can learn, reinforce, consolidate and then use as they move into Key Stage 2. This is discussed in more detail in the sections on additive and multiplicative reasoning.

Primary teachers are constantly reflecting on their teaching and wondering if they are doing a good job. Howe, Collier, McMahon, Earle and Davies, in their book *Science 5–11: A Guide for Teachers*, suggest criteria regarding what makes a good science teacher. Some of these criteria are appropriate and can be adapted for the teaching of mathematics.

Good mathematics teachers

- have clear personal aims for mathematics teaching;
- have an understanding of the mathematics they are teaching;
- have an understanding of the big ideas in mathematics to see where learning is leading and to address misconceptions as they arise;
- have an understanding of how the big ideas in mathematics relate to each other and to the other topics taught in the national curriculum for mathematics;
- value children's existing ideas and encourage them to share these with each other and you;
- have a repertoire of teaching strategies that children can use responsively and creatively;
- encourage the use of concrete materials and visual representations to develop understanding;
- feel excited about teaching mathematics.

This book aims to give guidance on how we, as teachers, can develop a complete, interconnected package of mathematical knowledge and understanding for the children we teach from the Early Years to Year 6.

I reference the national curriculum throughout, however not necessarily in the order that the requirements appear. All are covered throughout the primary years but have been adjusted to make a more coherent 'package' that can be presented to the children in an order that most can achieve a depth of understanding that is required for them to make good progress.

I have given a great deal of thought about how to set this book out. There are five major themes involved, each of which has many elements. Writing a coherent book would be difficult if I had to divide the pages into contrived chapters. So, rather than chapters, this book is set out in five main sections:

- Number sense
- Numerical reasoning
- Additive reasoning
- Multiplicative reasoning
- Geometric reasoning

Within each section are subsections which look at the various elements of the main section headings in more detail. Throughout runs a thread of how they link together. Also, the links that can be made within these key areas and measurement and statistics are looked at.

I hope that you enjoy reading this book and that you find it helpful!

References

Charles, R, Big ideas and understandings as the foundation for elementary and middle school mathematics, *Journal of Mathematics Education Leadership*, 2005, 7 (3), 9–24.

Howe, C, McMahon, E, & Davies, D, *Science 5–11: A guide for teachers*, David Fulton, United Kingdom, 2017.

Hurst, C & Hurrell, D, Developing the big ideas of number, *International Journal of Educational Studies in Mathematics*, 2014, 1 (2), 1–18.

NCETM, https://www.ncetm.org.uk/resources/50042, 2018.

Ross, S, *Place value: Problem solving and written assessment*, California State University, Long Beach, California, 1989.

Siemon, D, *Assessment for common misunderstandings: Introducing the big ideas 1*, RMIT University, Melbourne, Australia, 2006.

1

Number sense

This section includes:

- Counting
- Ordinal numbers
- Nominal numbers
- Comparing numbers
- Estimating
- Developing a sense of magnitude
- Composition of numbers
- Subitising
- Numbers to 12
- Connecting quantities to numbers and numerals
- Odd and even numbers
- Mathematical games

Introduction

Number sense

Number sense refers to 'a well organised conceptual framework of number information that enables a person to understand numbers and number relationships and to solve mathematical problems that are not bound by traditional algorithms' (Bobis 1996).

Knowing about, and having a sense of, number develops the skills which enable children to advance further in their mathematical understanding. We continue needing a sense of number when approaching new skills or concepts throughout our learning of mathematics. So, it is not something that children acquire in the early years of their education and not consider again in later years. Number sense is essential for all mathematical understanding. For example, when children encounter decimals, they need to have a sense of what decimal numbers are. They need to be able to count in decimal steps; they need to be able to compare them, know their composition, how they relate to one another and so on.

This section is therefore relevant to all phases in primary school, so please be sure to read it!

Over the years, various educational researchers have explored what they consider to be meant by number sense. I think the three key aspects that Sue Gifford, Jenni Back and Rose Griffiths refer to in their book *Making Numbers: Using Manipulatives to Teach Arithmetic* are simple and sum up what number sense is in a really helpful way:

1   Counting

2   Comparing

3   Composition

Counting

Children need to know the number names in order, first forwards and then backwards. They need to be able to understand how to count objects, events and actions, first, in ones and, then, in twos, fives and tens, other multiples and fractions, including decimals. Counting activities continue throughout primary school with increasing complexity.

In the 1970s, Gelman and Gallistell (1978) researched how children learn to count. The progression they developed is well known and still relevant now, decades later. This progression is called the Counting Principles; there are five:

1   The 1:1 principle: the ability to assign one number name to one object in the correct order and touch each object only once.

2   The stable order principle: knowing that numbers come in a particular order and being able to count consistently in that order. The numbers a child counts to in order may begin with just a few, but this will steadily increase over time, with practice.

3   The cardinal principle: the ability to count in order, understand the 1:1 principle and gradually notice that the final number in the count tells them how many there are in the group or set.

4   The abstract principle: knowing that anything can be counted, for example, objects, sounds, actions, words.

5   The order-irrelevance principle: understanding that in counting a group of objects, it does not matter where the objects are placed. This principle links to Piaget's conservation of number, where an amount remains constant even when its appearance has changed. For example, children can count a line of objects and tell you that there are eight. They can tell you that there are still eight when the objects are positioned in two rows of four or covered so none can be seen. Children develop their understanding that the number of objects remains the same because none have been added and none have been taken away. This is often a sticking point for children in the Early Years Foundation Stage (EYFS). To help them with this principle, children need plenty of practice.

I am by no means in the same league as Gelman and Gallistell, but I actually like to rearrange these principles so that the stable order principle comes first because I believe that children need to know the number order first in order to succeed in the 1:1 principle. I also like to place the order-irrelevance principle before the abstract principle because it is so important and because when children have mastered this principle, they are then in a position to be able to count anything.

My preferred order in these principles is

1 the stable order principle;
2 the 1:1 principle;
3 the cardinal principle;
4 the order-irrelevance principle;
5 the abstract principle.

I hope that these two esteemed gentlemen will forgive me!

In an ideal world, children should have mastered these counting skills by the time they leave Reception. They will not be able to develop other skills in number sense if they cannot count. I often suggest that teachers assess their children's ability to count, initially the stable order principle, in the Early Years and work with one or two children for a few minutes each day to practise counting to three, then four and so on until they can count competently to ten. Often, counting is carried out as a whole-class activity, which is good in many ways but is not necessarily the best way for all children. Some children in a class will be able to count, so for them, practising daily is probably unnecessary. Other children in the class will be in the very early stages of counting and may not be able to get past three, and they are likely to mumble the rest of the numbers inaccurately, so whole-class counting, if that is all that is done, is of little benefit to them. Small focus groups are possibly the best idea. Several teachers I know do this, and they say that it has had a massive impact. This idea works for all the counting principles. One Reception teacher told me that she had six children who had not mastered the 1:1 principle by the summer term of Year R. So, she spent a few minutes every day for a week with them, practising this skill, and by the end of the week, they had mastered it.

A few years ago, I carried out an assessment of 14 Reception children on their ability to count. I wanted to assess Gelman and Gallistell's 1:1, cardinal and order-irrelevance principles. I set out eight little men in a line. All the children could tell me that there were eight, so they had achieved the first two of these principles. I then moved two men so there was a row of two and a row of six. All the children had to count them again, apart from one little girl who said, 'Eight obviously.' I then moved another two so that there were rows of two, four and two. All the children had to count again, except the one little girl who said, 'Eight obviously.' I then scooped them all into my hands, and all the children said there were none, even when I opened my hands to show them. They could not see any, so therefore there were 'none'! The one little girl, again, said, 'Eight obviously.' I asked her why she kept saying, 'Eight obviously', and she said, 'Well, you haven't taken any away or added any to them so obviously there must be eight.' Both her reasoning and explanation were great. That is where we would like all EYFS children to be by the end of Reception. I suspect that little girl has the potential to go far in her mathematics.

Young children like hearing and saying big numbers. So, if they can count in units of 1 to 10, they can count in units of 10 to ten hundred (some will know that ten hundred is equivalent to 1000), they can count in units of 1000, 1 million, 1 billion and 1 trillion. The principle of counting is the same no matter what we are counting. This can make counting more fun. I have seen children really excited when counting in these 'big' numbers to ten of a particular unit.

Counting in units of different measurements is also helpful so that children can use the abstraction principle from Gelman and Gallistell's counting principles and understand that counting in centimetres, metres, kilograms, pence, pounds, minutes and so on works in the same way as counting numbers.

Children need to be able to count out a certain number of items from a larger group. I have seen teachers hold a handful of counters and ask the children to take five, counting as they do. When the child counts the fifth one, the rest are taken away! We cannot therefore assess whether children can do this because they have to stop counting as there are no more to count. We need to be mindful that we should keep the counters there so that we know whether the child has understood that they have taken five.

After 10, the children have to learn 11, 12 and the teens numbers. I call them the 'blah, blah' numbers. These are really tricky, and many children struggle with them. With a number like 14, at least you can hear that there must be a four in it somewhere. What about 13 and 15? *Thir* and *fif* do not sound much like *three* and *five*. In addition to pronouncing these numbers, young children often muddle the teens and tens numbers, saying, for example, 30 when they mean 13.

At the time of writing this book, I was trying out matching cards for the numbers 13 to 19 and 30 to 90, such as the following example, with children who have difficulty recognising and saying them correctly. First, the children sort the cards into all those that end with *teen* and all those ending with *ty*. They then pair them, a 'teen' card with the similar 'ty' card. Finally, take one pair and use manipulatives, such as Dienes or Numicon (published by Oxford University Press) to represent both numbers. In this way, they can see that, for example, 13 is made from one 10 and three 1s and that 30 is made from three 10s. They then do the same for another pair and then another. This is also a useful resource to display and make frequent reference to in the classroom.

Diagram 1.1

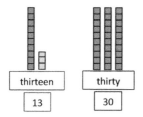
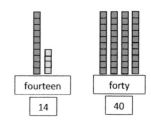

Interestingly, some schools using these cards are finding them very helpful, and some are already telling me that they are making a difference for some children because they can see the difference between the pairs of numbers and how they are made up. The visual clues of seeing the numbers in numerals and words and in quantities enable children to make verbal comparisons, and this aids their understanding.

Ordinal numbers

So far, we have thought about the cardinal aspect of counting; we also need to consider ordinal and nominal numbers. Ordinal numbers refer to the numbers in their positions when relating them to other numbers. We often begin teaching this by, for example, lining children or objects up and referring to number one in the line as first, the second in the line as second and so on. This example links to one to one correspondence as we are counting one item at a time, and they follow the stable order principle. When children begin ordering non-sequential numbers, such as 45, 67 and 98, we are referring their position compared with other numbers in that group. So, if ordering from the lowest number to the highest, 45 would be first in the order, 67 second and 98 third. Children should be thinking about how much greater, in this example, 67 is than 45 and how much less 67 is than 98.

The numbers children order become more complex as they go through primary school, for example, 3046, 3078, 3101, 3167, 3047. In this example, the digit in the thousands position remains the same, so consideration must be given, first, to the 100s; then, for 3046, 3078 and 3047, the 10s; and, finally, for 3046 and 3047, the 1s.

Number lines are really useful tools for representing ordinal numbers. Initially, by using number tracks and then numbered number lines, children can identify the positions of numbers and see the numbers that come before and after. These tools are also helpful for finding one or two more or less than a given number. They are essential pieces of equipment for young children. When ready, they move onto using partially numbered number lines so that they can identify missing numbers and then onto empty number lines with parameters. Finally, children should be able to draw their own. At this stage, they will use their reasoning skills to decide their own start and end points for their line and then mark different numbers.

Using number lines to find the difference between numbers by counting on or back is a helpful mental calculation strategy that we should encourage the children to develop. As with many areas of number sense, using number lines for positioning numbers and finding totals and differences does not stop in Key Stage 1; it continues into Key Stage 2 for larger numbers, negative numbers and decimals. The National Numeracy Strategy (NNS) developed Interactive Teaching Programmes for many areas of mathematics, and number lines were one. The programmes have now been archived but are still available. Of course, you can find many on the internet, but best of all, develop your own so that they are pertinent to the needs of your children.

Number track

1	2	3	4	5	6	7	8	9	10

We could give children instructions and ask questions, for example,

> Put four teddies on the number track. Count them as you do. Why have you positioned your teddies there? Is there another way? Which is the best way? Why?
>
> How many more do you need to make five? How do you know?
>
> What about six? Seven? Eight? How do you know?
>
> What do you notice?

The following are some examples of number lines from the NNS with a few questions to get the children thinking.

> Where is 6?
>
> What number is one less than 6? What number is one more than 6? Explain how you know using the number line.
>
> What is the difference between 3 and 5? How did you work that out? Is there another way you could have done that? Which do you think is the easiest? Why?

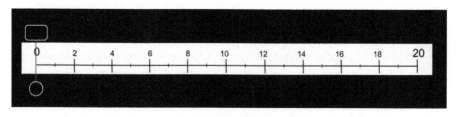

> Where would 13 be positioned on this number line? How do you know? How else do you know?
>
> What about 15? What is one less/more than 15? How do you know?

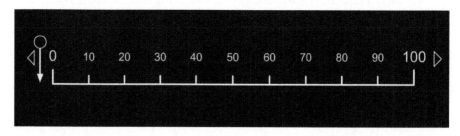

> Where would 62 be positioned on this number line? What multiples of 10 would it be positioned on either side? Why? Is it closer to 60 or 70? How do you know?

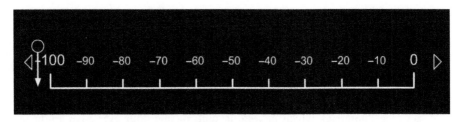

What is a negative number? What can you tell me about negative numbers? Where do we see negative numbers in real life? Is negative 16 closer to negative 20 or negative 10? What would happen if we added 10 onto negative 45? What would happen if we subtracted 6 from negative 30?

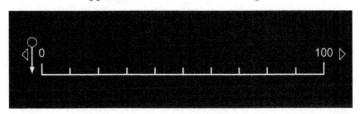

What does each division represent? By how many do these intervals increase? Where would 91 be positioned? What about 11? Is 91 closer to 100, or is 11 closer to zero? How do you know?

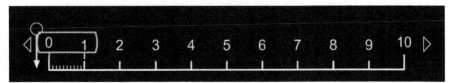

What is the value of each division shown between 0 and 1? Where would 4 tenths be positioned? How else can you represent 4 tenths? Can you tell me a number that comes between 6 and 7? Can you tell me another? And another? What are the values of these numbers? Can you tell me in two different ways?

Nominal numbers

Nominal numbers are numbers used for labelling. Numbering things in the classroom or around school, for example, the pegs that children hang their coats on, is a good practice. This concept overlaps with ordinal numbers because the labelling of pegs usually goes in an ordinal sequence. Randomly numbering trays or boxes of resources is a good idea because this does not necessarily imply an ordinal sequence. For example, asking a child to find the box of, for example, mathematics games, with the numeral 3 written on it is helpful. This also reinforces number recognition. Adding the number word and a visual clue, such as a picture of that number of items, a collection of real items or a Numicon plate, is also helpful.

Nominal numbers often appear when we are working with measurement. The numbers tell us how many units there are of a particular quantity, for example, 10 mm, 23 cm,

4 m, 15 km, 600 g, 5 kg, 400 ml, 8 l. The height of a child, for example, would be a nominal number; it is a label indicating the child's height at that particular time.

Analogue clocks are both ordinal and nominal. The hour numbers are in order and giving the number of the hour is nominal but these change over time and are therefore also ordinal. They also indicate five-minute intervals, which are nominal but as they change they are ordinal. Digital clocks are similar: the numbers on the left show hours as a label (nominal), which increase in units of one hour over a day (ordinal), and the numbers on the right show minutes as a label (nominal), which increase in units of one minute over an hour (ordinal).

Comparing

Comparing involves having a feel for the relative sizes of number, for example, knowing that 7 is greater than 3 but less than 10. Once children are able to compare pairs of numbers, they can then put three or more numbers in order. As with counting, this area of number sense continues throughout Key Stages 1 and 2 as children order, for example, three-, then four- and five-digit numbers with one, two and then three decimal places.

Comparing also includes estimating. Estimating is a skill that some children find difficult, often because they want to know exact amounts and actual answers to calculations. They often think that if they give an answer that is not exact, they are incorrect. They need to develop the belief that if an estimate is within given parameters then they are good estimators. It is important that we give children plenty of opportunities to estimate from an early age so it becomes another skill that they just 'do'. The next part of this section goes into more detail on estimating.

Simply showing dots in a completely random order helps with this.

Diagram 1.2

Once children have estimated, showing the dots in an easily recognisable pattern, like those seen on dice or dominoes, can help them check their response.

Showing easily recognisable patterns moves children from the additive approach (counting every item) to the multiplicative approach (using known multiples). Another idea for helping with the multiplicative approach is to encourage the children to count in multiples of 2, 3, 4 and so on instead of counting one at a time. As they count in multiples, they move groups of that multiple away from the main body of items. Any remaining items that do not make a group can then be counted individually.

Introducing symbols to show whether numbers are greater than, less than or equal to is a shorthand for words. These can be introduced to children in the EYFS when comparing pairs of numbers. Some teachers use 'crocodiles' and tell children that the crocodile eats the big number. Some teachers think this is helpful for children. It is not! Children do not come into school thinking that crocodiles eat 'big' numbers; this is a misconception that we introduce to them. We need to use precise mathematical vocabulary and symbols. Crocodiles do not eat numbers; they only eat meat! So we should not encourage this misconception.

Other countries use models, such as those that follow, which are far more accurate. Fortunately, more and more teachers in this country are moving away from 'crocodiles' and using mathematical visualisations similar to these.

Diagram 1.3

4 is greater than 2   2 is less than 4   3 is equal to 3

After deciding whether a number is greater or less than another number, encouraging children to find out, using manipulatives, how to make numbers equal is a good idea. For example, $45 > 38, 38 < 45, 45 - 7 = 38, 45 = 38 + 7$.

The symbol for equality is very important. It means that what is on one side is equal to, the same as or equivalent to what is on the other. Many children view the equal-to symbol as a symbol which indicates an answer is to follow. Recently, a colleague and I were talking to some Year 1 children. These children were completing a worksheet of addition calculations. My colleague was asking one child about the numbers and symbols on the sheet. She was able to tell him about the numbers and that the addition symbol meant that she had to add the numbers together. When he asked about the equal-to symbol, the girl said, 'That means the answer goes on the other side.' She is not alone in that thinking. I have come across Year 6 children with exactly the same misconception. To prevent this misconception from arising, we need to present the equal-to symbol in different positions, for example, $6 + 3 = 9, 9 = 6 + 3, 8 + 1 = 6 + 3$.

Numicon provides sets of balance scales which introduce the idea of equality through balancing. Children put one or more Numicon plates (which are weighted) in one pan and then experiment to find what they need to put into the other to make the pans balance. This opens opportunities for exploring many alternatives, for example, $8 + 3 = 7 + 4$ or $6 + 5$ or $3 + 3 + 4 + 1$ and so on. This is a great start for developing an understanding of equivalence.

We should, therefore, be precise about the equal-to symbol from the beginning so that we do not lead children into thinking that after this symbol there is an answer! This misconception is easily avoidable.

Estimating

To estimate means to find something close to the correct answer. In other words, you are approximating. For example, on 24 November 2017, BBC News announced that 'women in England and Wales are having 1.9 children on average, fewer than their mothers who had 2.2 offspring, according to the Office for National Statistics'. Obviously, nobody can have 1.9 or 2.2 children, so we make an approximation. We usually do this by rounding to make both numbers 2 – not accurate and not a reflection of the fact that women had fewer children in 2017 but an estimate nonetheless. There is more information on rounding in the Numerical Reasoning section of this book. Because children tend to like being precise, we need to give them opportunities where estimating is essential.

With younger children, I play a game called 'Play Your Cards Right' (basically copying the idea of the television game show). I present them with a series of cards, one at a time, with dots randomly placed on them, and they estimate the number of dots; we then count them, and then they predict whether the next card will have more or fewer dots. The dots range from 1 to 20 on the cards. The following are some examples.

Diagram 1.4

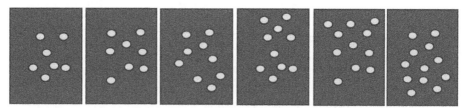

The dots are arranged so that, when counting to check their estimate, the children can subitise (knowing the number without counting) some of the dots to move the counting process away from counting every dot individually. On the first card, they may be able to subitise the two dots and the four dots, so giving six, and then they can add on the other one. On the last card, they may subitise the top four dots, then the three on the left-hand side to give seven dots and then count on in ones for the remaining five. Children will not always subitise the same groups of dots, so it is worth asking them the different ways in which they do this. The game ends when they can correctly predict five cards in a row.

An activity I do with older children is to give them a bar chart like the one that follows, created using the NNS's Interactive Teaching Programme 'bar graphs and pie charts'.

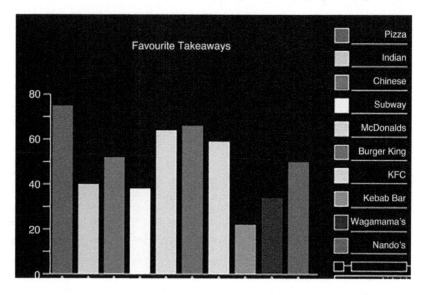

The bar chart has a problem to go with it: 'Akemi is planning a takeaway party. She wants to choose some takeaways that her friends will like. She carried out a survey. Which five should she choose?'

The children are given a few minutes to estimate the number of people voting for each takeaway food. They have to estimate because the scale increases in multiples of 10 and there is no individual division. I also show it on a whiteboard, so they are a distance away from it. Obviously, the answer to the problem can be achieved by simply looking at the heights of the bars, but we want to attach a number to each food. For example, for pizza, the number of people is between 70 and 80, possibly 75, so that would make a good estimate. The Indian choice is selected by just under 40 people, so a good estimate might be 39. Once they have made their estimates, we reveal the actual numbers.

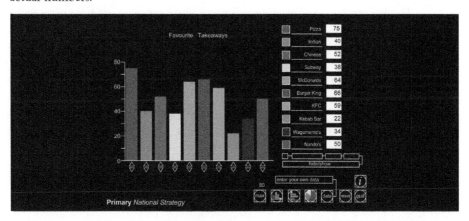

I ask them to circle the estimates they made that were completely accurate. They then look at their other estimates, and if they were two or three numbers on either side of the actual figures, we say that their estimates were pretty good. Interestingly, the children's first instinct was to put a cross beside those that were not completely accurate, even if they were good estimates!

We then ask questions about the data, and children use mental calculation strategies to answer. For example, when asked, 'How many people voted for Chinese and Subway?' hopefully, they would use, for example, number pairs to 10: $2 + 8 = 10, 50 + 30 + 10 = 90$. We ask difference questions as well, such as 'How many more people voted for Pizza than for KFC?' Hopefully they would use a rounding, a counting on or a making subtraction easier strategy to find the difference between 75 and 59. Mental calculation strategies for addition and subtraction are looked at in more depth in the Additive Reasoning section.

This is also a good opportunity to link number skills with statistics.

Providing other things that need estimating, such as a jar of sweets, a bag of potatoes or jigsaw puzzles to estimate quantities and shopping receipts to estimate costs in money, are helpful in encouraging children to become confident estimators.

The important message here is that estimating is often all we can do unless we have the opportunity to be accurate, so we need to help children develop this skill.

Developing a sense of magnitude

Another aspect of comparing numbers involves developing a sense of magnitude, which is basically having a feel for how large something is. Can the children tell you that a pile of 20 cubes is greater than a pile of 10 without counting? They should be able to do this by simply looking and making the judgement that there appears to be more cubes in the pile of 20. Of course, they would need to count to check their thinking! Regularly giving children opportunities for working on these types of activities is important; for example, you could show two groups of different numbers of items on a whiteboard and ask which has the greatest number and which has the least. This could naturally lead to estimating the number in each group and then counting to check and so encourage the development of a sense of magnitude.

Developing a sense of magnitude is particularly pertinent when it comes to measurement in both Key Stage 1 and Key Stage 2. Children need to be able to tell you that, for example, an apple has a mass closer to one gram than one kilogram; that a bucket of water would be measured in litres, not millilitres; that the distance across the school playground would be measured in metres, not centimetres. If children cannot tell you this, it is because they have not had sufficient practice in dealing with measurement in practical ways.

Think back to Piaget and his theory of conservation; he spoke about the conservation of measurement as well as number. Many children think that because something is larger in size, it must be heavier; if a container is taller than another, it must have a greater capacity. Some children will think a length of string when scrunched into a ball will now be shorter than when it was stretched to show its full length. This is similar to the order-irrelevance principle in counting in that, if it looks different, it must be different! Practical measurement activities will help children understand that, as with number, this is not necessarily true.

When dealing with mass, we need to give children the opportunity to feel objects and compare them with a 1 kg weight or something with that mass so that they begin to develop a feel for 1 kg and can compare items against it. We need to make available items of different shapes and sizes that have the same mass, so that they begin to understand that the size of an object is not necessarily relative to its mass. They need to be able to identify items that are less than, greater than and the same as 1 kg initially and then other masses, for example 500 g and 2 kg.

We need to provide similar activities for length; for example, when we show the children what 1 m looks like with a metre stick and what 30 cm looks like using a school ruler, we give them something to base their estimates and measurements of length. They can then compare and contrast different items according to these parameters. We need to show the same lengths in different ways, for example, a straight line drawn on paper alongside a curvy line and a zigzag line of the same length. In this way, children will be able to see that the appearance of the lines bears no relevance to the actual length. We often show a series of straight lines for the children to measure and order. The order of the lengths is obvious because all the lines are the same, just shorter or longer. We therefore need to give examples that are not so obvious and that will cause them to reason about the lengths. We also need to give children opportunities for estimating different lengths, using a metre stick and ruler as a guide to help them make sensible estimates.

Capacity is another area of measurement which is tricky to estimate. Children often think that the capacity of a tall container is greater than that of a shorter but wider container. Again, they need plenty of practical experiences of filling different-sized containers with the same volume of water so that they develop the understanding that the appearance of a container has no bearing on its capacity. Showing 500 ml, 1 litre and 2 litre bottles is a good idea so that children can get a feel for these capacities. They should then be able to estimate and check, for example, which other containers these might fill.

Measurement comes as a separate section in the national curriculum after fractions. As a result it is usually treated as a separate area of mathematics, and often, insufficient time is given to it because of the pressure that other 'more important' concepts need to be taught. If we build practical measurement activities into the number-based work we do, we will have more time to focus on both areas of the curriculum and the children will have the chance to deepen their understanding of both and see the links between them.

Composition

Composition involves a developing understanding of how each number can be made up in different ways, for example, by adding and subtracting, multiplying and dividing. At school, children begin to develop their understanding of this in the Early Years. Introducing the concepts of commutativity and inverse as soon as children begin to add and subtract is important. If they know that $2 + 3 = 5$, they also know that $3 + 2 = 5$ because addition is commutative. Which way the numbers are added does not matter; the sum will always be the same. They also know that $5 - 3 = 2$ and $5 - 2 = 3$ because addition and subtraction are inverse operations. They begin to make the link that by subtracting the addend (the number we add) from the sum, the difference is the augend (the number we start with) and vice versa.

We should be aiming to help children develop visual imagery for numbers, to encourage mental flexibility and take them beyond the recognition of number names and numerals to include rich part–part–whole knowledge. For example, when children read, write or hear *eight*, they can imagine what that collection might look like and how it relates to other numbers. They may visualise 8 as 1 more than 7, 1 less than 9, greater than three, less than 12, double 4, 3 and 5, as even and so on. This is not about addition and subtraction at this stage; it is about deeply understanding what each number means (adapted from Siemon 2006).

Drawing visual images to support this is helpful. Many teachers use a circular part–whole model. This should go alongside the bar model.

Diagram 1.5

Some teachers believe the numbers in a bar model need to be of proportional size. I agree that for fractions, this is important, but for number pairs, I do not think it is necessary. It often proves a distraction. Children frequently use the circle model in EYFS and Year 1. The circles are the same size no matter what the number. If we want children to be introduced to the idea of the bar model alongside this, then the bars can be the same size. I guess this is a personal preference. My thinking is that we want the children to focus on what we are teaching them, and therefore, they do not need added distractions of figuring out how big each part of the bar must be. I have observed lessons during which teachers wanted children to make each part proportional, and that element took over the main point of the lesson.

At a later stage, children should be able to break numbers up to make addition simpler; for example, 26 + 18 could be seen as 20 + 10 + 10 + 4 or 30 + 14. This is the distributive law for addition and requires an element of reasoning. Many mental calculation strategies depend on children being flexible in their thinking of how to use numbers to simplify calculations. We need to help children become flexible thinkers. This is focused on in more depth in the section on additive reasoning.

Composition also involves an increasing understanding that our number system uses groups of 1000s, 100s, 10s, 1s, tenths and so on. Unitising plays a part here. Children need to be aware that 100 can be seen as 1 unit of 100 or 10 units of 10 or 100 units of 1. Children begin counting in units of one. They then count in units of 2, 5, 10 and then units of other multiples.

Subitising

Another important aspect of number sense is the skill of subitising. This is the ability to recognise a quantity without counting. Dice and domino activities are important in helping children learn to subitise numbers to 6. The patterns they form enable the children to know what numbers they represent without counting all the dots.

When given a random display of dots, they will develop the ability to subitise a group and count on from that. For example, in the pattern shown in the following, children might be able to subitise the three dots at the top and count on from 3. They might be able to subitise the 4 or 5 at the bottom and count on from that. They might be able to subitise and know that 3 and 4 make 7 and that there is just one more to add.

Diagram 1.6

This highlights the importance of planning our examples carefully, to lead children into their learning and understanding is key. If we do not provide opportunities for children to spot these patterns these skills, for most children, will not develop and they will continue to count everything one by one, which is inefficient and can lead to errors.

Numbers to 12

In the EYFS classroom, there is an expectation that the children develop an understanding of all numbers to 10, but it makes sense to look at numbers to 12. The numbers 11 and 12 are kind of in a no-man's land as they are not within 10, but they are not 'teens' numbers. So recently, I decided to include them within the idea of numbers to 10. I encourage EYFS teachers whom I work with to focus on one number a week so that children have the opportunity to explore a particular number in a variety of different contexts, including those in real life. These contexts include length, mass, capacity, volume, money and time. These contexts provide rich opportunities for exploring numbers and allow the teacher to find out what children already know from their experiences outside school by using a set of slides and ideas for the activities. These could be explored as a whole class, during guided group activities or a mixture of both.

To begin, I show all the pictures and just ask the children to tell me what they can see. This can be a revelation as some children can tell you a great deal about what they see that is quite unexpected – again from their experiences outside school.

The following are examples for the numbers 1 to 3.

Number 1

For number 1, make up a slide with images of:

- Large numeral 1
- Hand with one finger pointing
- Number line like the one below

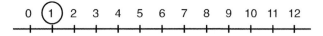

- Numicon one plate
- One written in words
- 1st birthday card
- 1p coin
- £1 coin
- Domino with one dot
- Dice showing one dot
- Horizontal line
- Vertical line
- 1 o'clock shown on an analogue clock
- 1:00 shown on a digital clock
- One litre bottle of water
- 1kg dumb bell
- Metre stick
- Ruler showing centimetres
- Birthday cake with one candle
- Skittle

Number 1: Ask children to draw 1 in the air, on someone's back, on paper, on a whiteboard, in sand, in water and so on.

Number line: Discuss the position of 1 on the number line, which number does it follow? What number is after 1? What number is two more than 1.

The word one: It is important that the children become familiar with what numbers look like in both numerals and word. There is no need to do anything but familiarise the children with the word one.

The finger: Ask children to show one finger and then another one. How many different ways can they show one finger? Talk about the different fingers: index, middle, ring and little. Ask children to show each one on each hand. What if they include thumbs? Talk about what a thumb is and how it is the same as and different from a finger. Do they notice that all the fingers have three joints but that the thumb has two? It is also shorter and wider than the other fingers. Thumbs and fingers are all digits and found on a hand.

The birthday card: Ask children to tell you how many years a child needs to be alive to be given this card. Talk about the ages in the classroom and ask them to tell you how many years ago it was when they were one. They could do this using their fingers. Put a thumb up for 1 and then the three fingers to make 4 or four to make 5. Those fingers show the difference between 1 and 4 or 5.

The penny: Give each child a 1 pence coin. Referring to coins and small amounts of money as pence, for example, 1 pence rather than 1p, is important; we can write the amount as 1p, but we must not verbally refer to it as one p. A pea is a small green vegetable that we eat, so we must refer to money as pence. What do they notice about the one pence coin? What shape is it: cylindrical with two circular faces. What pictures are there on each side? What is it? Agree that it is money. Could we buy anything for one penny? Agree that no, we would need lots of 1 pence coins to buy something. You could talk about how a long time ago you could buy, for example, sweets for one penny. Ask children to make a rubbing of the penny with wax crayons. The rubbing could be cut out and used to make a collage for the number one. Hide pennies in the sand and water trays and ask children to see how quickly they can find or retrieve them. How many did they find in, for example, one minute?

The pound coin: Repeat the preceding activity for the £1 coin. This is an interesting shape. It is a prism with faces of 12 sides (dodecagons). How is it similar to a one pence coin? How is it different?

The vertical line: Ask children to draw a vertical line in the air, in sand, in water and so on. Ensure that you call it a vertical line. Children are never too young to be introduced to the correct vocabulary. You could ask them to draw a vertical line on paper. Encourage them to do this using a ruler – no measurement required!

The horizontal line: Repeat the preceding ideas for a horizontal line. What could they do to the horizontal line to make it vertical and vice versa? Discuss the fact that they could turn each one quarter of a turn to make the other.

They could try this out using their drawing of a vertical line. How can they make it horizontal?

The dumbbell: Do the children know what one of these is? Explain that it is something that people use to help their muscles grow. Talk about muscles and their purpose. Explain that their main function is to help us move. They are the only part of the body that can contract to move other parts of the body. You could ask them to try and feel the muscles in their arms. Another purpose is to enable us to stand up straight, lie down, sit and so on. Ask children to identify what is written on the dumbbell. Establish that 1 kg is the mass of the dumbbell. Have some things that weigh 1 kg, for example, a 1 kg weight or 1 kg bag of sugar, bag of rice, bag of potatoes and so on, available. Give children the opportunity to hold them to get a feel for the weight of 1 kg. Can they find objects in the classroom that weigh less than 1 kg, greater than 1 kg and about the same? Ask them to compare what they have selected with 1 kg on balance scales. Children need to begin to use the word *mass* instead of *weight* in Year 2. It is worth introducing this word from the beginning.

The cake: Have a discussion about favourite cakes and sweets. You could turn this into a simple statistics activity by making a tally of a set of about eight choices.

The ruler: Give each child a ruler. Ask the children to tell you what it is and what it is used for. Talk about things that can be measured. Establish that it is for measuring short objects and drawing short lines. Ask them to look carefully at it and to tell you what they notice. The children should be able to tell you that there are marks and numbers on the ruler. Ask them if they know what the numbers represent. Establish that the distance from one number to the next is 1 cm. Ask them to use the ruler to draw different lines. Then ask them to draw a line of 1 cm. Can they find anything in the classroom that is shorter than 1 cm? Ask them to make a collection of things that are longer than 1 cm.

The metre stick: Repeat the preceding activity with a metre stick. Include measuring the children's heights. Are they taller or shorter than 1 m? What can they find that is shorter than a metre?

Domino: Do children know what a domino is and what they would do with it? Briefly explain the game of dominoes. How many dots can they see? Give small groups a set of dominoes and ask them to identify all the dominoes that have one dot on one or both sides. How many are there? Ask them to pair them up so that the ones match.

Numicon plate: Give each child a one Numicon plate. What can they tell you about it? Agree on the colour and the fact that there is one hole. Establish that it represents one. Give the children the opportunity to make pictures and patterns with several Numicon 1 plates. They could draw their patterns on paper by drawing around each plate.

Dice: Can children tell you what this is? Agree that it is a dice. Ask them when and why they might use a dice. Sadly, not all families play games together that involve dice, so some children may have never seen one before. What other numbers would they find on this dice? Give pairs a dice and ask them to throw it and count the number of throws until they throw a one. Who throws a one first? Demonstrate this for them first.

Skittle: Ask children if they know what it is and how the game is played. Give the children the opportunity to try to knock a skittle down with a large, soft ball. How many throws does it take to knock the skittle down? Encourage them to record how many throws in their own way. Build on this over time, for example, adding a skittle for each new number focused on. The game is played with a total of 10 skittles. When you get to number 10, teach a group of children how to play the game. They could record the number knocked down by matching with a Numicon plate and then recording that number in their own way.

Bottle of water: Show the children a real 1 litre bottle of water. What can they tell you about it? Do they know that liquid is measured in litres? If not, share this with them to familiarise them with this unit. Discuss what could be measured in litres. Give them the opportunity to fill 1 litre bottles with water. Can they fill a bottle half full? Can they order bottles from empty to half full to full? Use this opportunity to discuss what is meant by half. Can they fill other containers with 1 litre of water?

Clocks: Have any of the children seen both types of clock? These days, children are likely to be more familiar with digital time. Do they know what clocks are for? Can anyone tell you what time the clocks show? Discuss the two hands on the analogue clock and what they show. Talk about the minute marks and the hour numbers. Emphasise that the time is 1 o'clock. The minute hand points to the 12 and the hour hand to the 1. If possible, ask children to show this time on a clock of their own. Focus on the digital time. Where have children seen this before? Point out that the number 1 tells the hour and the two zeros show that there are no minutes past, so this time also shows 1 o'clock. Talk about the differences and similarities between the digital and analogue clocks. You could spend some time thinking about the units of time and how long they are. Clap to indicate a second. Ask them to close their eyes for one minute. What could they do in one minute? Try out some activities.

Number 2

For number 2, make up a slide with images of:

- Large numeral 2
- Two hands with thumbs pointing up
- Number line like the one below

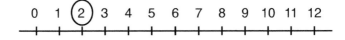

- Numicon two plate
- Two written in words
- 2ⁿᵈ birthday card
- Two 1p coins
- 2p coin
- Two £1 coins
- £2 coin
- Domino with two dots
- Dice showing two dots
- The horizontal and vertical lines from number 1 joined together to make a right angle
- 2 o'clock shown on an analogue clock
- 2:00 shown on a digital clock
- Two litre bottle of water
- 2kg dumb bell
- Metre stick
- Birthday cake with two candles

Number 2: Ask children to draw a 2 in the air, on someone's back, on whiteboards, on paper, in sand, in water and so on. Establish that 2 is the number that comes after 1.

Number line: Discuss the position of 2 on the number line, which number does it follow? What number is after 2? What number is two more than 2.

The word two: Simply familiarise the children with the word two.

The two thumbs: Ask children if they can remember what is different about thumbs and fingers. Recap this. Can they put both thumbs up and hide the other fingers? Can they show two using their thumbs and fingers in different ways? How many different ways can they find? There are lots of ways!

Two pennies and the 2 pence coin: Can children remember what the 1 pence coin is? Recap this. How many 1 pence coins can they see? Do they know that two 1 pence coins are the same value as a 2 pence coin? Spend time on this equivalence. You could ask them to say, 'Two pennies are equivalent to one two-pence coin.' Give them 1 pence and 2 pence coins. They exchange two 1 pence coins for a 2 pence coin. Keep doing this until no 1 pence coins are left. Ask them what addition statement they could make: 1 p + 1 p = 2 p. Ask children to make a rubbing of the 2 pence coin with wax crayons. These rubbings could be cut out and used in a collage to make a large number 2. Hide pennies in the sand and water trays and ask children to see how quickly they can find or retrieve them and group them in twos to make a value of 2 pence. How many did they collect? They could then exchange these pairs of pennies for 2 pence coins.

Two pounds and the £2 coin: Repeat the preceding activity with pound coins.

Cake: Can children tell you why they think the cake is there? Agree that it has two candles. What do they think this means? Agree possibly a birthday cake for a two-year-old. How many years ago were they two? As before they use two fingers and then find the difference between two and four or five. Can they describe the cake? As with the number one, you could make a list of their choices and draw a tally of the votes.

Dominoes: Why do they think the domino is on the slide? Agree two dots on each side. Can they count the total number of dots with you? Give small groups a set of dominoes and ask them to identify all the dominoes that have two dots on one or both sides. How many are there? Can they pair them up so that two dots match?

Numicon plate: Ask children how many holes are on a 1 plate. How is this plate different? Agree that it is a different colour and that it has two holes. Give children 1 and 2 plates and ask them to pair the 1 plates together to make two and place them on top of the 2 plate. What addition statement can they make: $1 + 1 = 2$. What happens if they take a 1s plate away? They could say that $2 - 1 = 1$. When you do this ensure you use the vocabulary add and subtract as these are the operational words that the children need to learn. Do this a few times and encourage volunteers to write the number statements on the board for the class to check. They could use these 1 and 2 plates to make patterns and then describe them to a friend.

Dice: What number can they see on the dice? How many more dots are on this compared to the dice with one dot? Give pairs a dice and ask them to throw it and count the number of throws until they throw a two. Who throws a two first? Demonstrate this for them first.

Clocks: Can they remember the time on the analogue clock for number 1? Where was the minute hand pointing? Where was the hour hand pointing? Where is it pointing this time? What time is it? What number was showing on the digital clock? What number is showing now? Discuss the fact that two o'clock is one hour after one o'clock.

Birthday card: Ask the children to describe the card. What age would a child be if he or she received this on his or her birthday? How many years older is two than one? Point to the word *two*. Can children tell you what it says? Hide the word and see if anyone can spell it.

2 kg dumbbells: What is the difference between this photograph and the one with the 1 kg dumbbell? Agree that this shows a dumbbell with a mass of 2 kg. Can the children tell you that two 1 kg dumbbells would be the same as the 2 kg dumbbells? Give children something that weighs 2 kg, for example, two bags of sugar or a 2 kg bag of potatoes, so that they get a feel for this mass. Can they find anything heavier than, lighter than and about the same as 2 kg in the classroom? Use balance scales as before to compare.

2 litre bottle of water: How is this bottle of water different to the 1 litre bottle of water on the previous slide? Agree that it holds 2 litre of water, so it must hold more and be bigger. It holds twice the amount. Discuss the fact that they would need two 1 litre bottles to give an equivalent amount of water. Give children the opportunity to fill 2 litre bottles full of water. Can they fill them half full? Introduce the word *capacity* as the amount the bottle will hold and *volume* as the amount in the bottle at a given time. How many containers can they fill using the 2 litre bottle?

Two lines: Can children remember the words *horizontal* and *vertical* from when they previously looked at these lines? If not remind them of these terms. Invite a volunteer to point to the horizontal line and another to point to the vertical line. What letter do the two lines make? Tell the children that the two lines meet at a right angle. Ask children to make a right angle using their arms, hands and fingers. Can they point out right angles in the classroom? There will be lots!

Number 3

For number 3, make up a slide with images of:

- Large numeral 3
- One or two hands with three fingers pointing up
- Number line like the one below

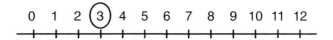

- Numicon three plate
- Three written in words
- 3rd birthday card
- Three 1p coins
- 1p coin and 2p coin
- Three £1 coins
- £2 coin and £1 coin
- Domino with three dots
- Dice showing three dots
- Three triangles, equilateral, isosceles and scalene
- 3 o'clock shown on an analogue clock
- 3:00 shown on a digital clock
- Toys in different arrangements of three
- Birthday cake with three candles

Number 3: Ask children to draw a 3 in the air, on someone's back, on a white-board, on paper, in sand, in water and so on. Emphasise that the number 3 comes after the number 2. How many more than 1 is 3?

Number line: Discuss the position of 3 on the number line, which number does it follow? What number is after 3? What number is two more than 3?

The word three: Familiarise the children with the word three.

The three fingers: Ask children to show three fingers in the same way. Can they show three using their thumbs and fingers in different ways using one hand and then both? How many different ways can they find? There are lots of ways!

Three pennies and the 2 pence and 1 pence coin: Can children remember how many 1 pence coins are equivalent to a 2 pence coin? Recap this. How many 1 pence coins can they see? Can they tell you how else they could make 3 pence? Point out the two coins on the slide. Give them 1 pence and 2 pence coins. They exchange two 1 pence coins for a 2 pence coin and then add another 1 pence to make a total of 3 pence. Keep doing this until there are no one pence coins left. Ask them what addition statement they could make: 1 p + 2 p = 3 p. If they know this, what else do they know: 2 p + 1 p = 3 p. Introducing commutativity as soon as the opportunity arises is important. Ask children to make a rubbing of both a 1 pence and a 2 pence coin with wax crayons. These rubbings could be cut out and used to make a collage of the number 3. Hide 1 pence and 2 pence coins in the sand and water trays and ask children to see how quickly they can find or retrieve one of each and group together to make 3 pence. How many collections of 3 pence did they make?

Three £1 coins and the £2 coin and £1: Repeat the preceding activities with pound coins.

Dominoes: Why do the children think the domino is on the slide? Agree that it has three dots on each side. Can they count the total number of dots with you? Give small groups a set of dominoes and ask them to identify all the dominoes that have three dots on one or both sides. How many are there? Can they pair them up so that the three dots match?

Numicon plate: Ask children how many holes is on a 1 plate. How many on a 2 plate? How is this plate different? Agree that it is a different colour and that it has three holes. Give children 1, 2 and 3 plates and ask them to pair the 1s and 2s plates to make 3 and place them on top of the 3 plate. What addition statements can they make: 1 + 2 = 3 and 2 + 1 = 3. What happens if they take a 1s plate away? They could say that 3 − 1 = 2. What happens if they take the 2s plate away? They could say that 3 − 2 = 1. Do this a few times and encourage volunteers to write the number statements on the board for the class to check. Is there another way they could make the 3s plate: 1 + 1 + 1 = 3? They could make patterns and pictures using the 3 plates to describe to a friend. Remember to use the vocabulary of add and subtract. Introduce the word *addition* for combining two numbers. Introduce the fact that it does not matter which way round two numbers are added, the answer will always by the same because addition is commutative. Introducing correct vocabulary is important. Children will become familiar with it, and some will be able to use it quickly while others will use it over time.

Dice: Can children tell you what number the dice show? How do they know? Give pairs a dice and ask them to throw it and count the number of throws until they throw a 3. Who throws a 3 first? Ask them to think about how could they throw a 3 with two dice. Reinforce the fact 1 + 2 = 3 and 2 + 1 = 3.

Clocks: Can children remember the time on the analogue clock for number 1 and number 2? Where was the minute hand pointing? Where is it pointing to this time (same number)? Where was the hour hand pointing on both clocks? Where is it pointing this time? What time is it? What number was showing on the digital clock for both times? What number is showing now? Discuss the fact that three o'clock is one hour after two o'clock. How many hours is it after one o'clock?

Birthday card: Ask the children to describe the card. What age would a child be if he or she received this on his or her birthday? How many years older is 3 than 1 and 2? How many years ago did they receive a card with a 3 on it? Can the children read any of the words on the card?

Triangles: Ask the children what is the same and what is different about them. Agree that they all have three sides and three corners but that the lengths of their sides are different. Do they know the name of the shapes? As a class, make the generalisation that any three-sided shape is a triangle. Say together, 'All three-sided shapes are called triangles.'

The slides continue in a similar way for all numbers to 12 ensuring the use of analogue and digital clocks and regular and irregular shapes. Of course, with shapes, we must introduce the correct vocabulary. For example, for the number 4, the children see two different quadrilaterals and are introduced to that word, which, for some reason, does not appear in the national curriculum until Key Stage 2. However, it is the name for any four-sided shape and needs to be introduced as soon as four-sided shapes arise.

I have introduced these slides to 10 and more recently 12 and the guidance that accompanies them to many nursery and Reception teachers. The teachers using them tell me that they are very successful. Children can read o'clock times on analogue and digital clocks by the time they get to number 12 and can find o'clock times on analogue clocks. This is not an outcome for the Early Years, but I look at this as an added bonus and a prelude for what they need to learn about in future as well as a real-life skill. Because telling o'clock times on analogue and digital clocks is not an early learning goal, if some children do not achieve this, it does not matter, but, as with substituting pennies for different coins, for children who can, this activity provides an extra challenge, and some children in EYFS need challenging. The work from these slides enables children to begin understanding the concept of commutativity. One teacher told me that when children in her class were looking at the number 6, one boy immediately said that the £5 note and the £1 coin must make £6 because 5 add 1 equals 6. Connections are being made!

The Reception teachers at Georgian Gardens gave me the following feedback: 'We have noticed that with regards to number understanding, the gap between the less able and the more able has decreased. The children have a much deeper understanding of what each number means i.e. the sixness of six.'

Teachers in Year 1 at Georgian Gardens have carried out similar activities, looking at a number a day. As a class, they explored different ways to represent numbers to 10. The children then went on to show their own ways to represent them through their own drawings.

The following is an example of one child's representation of the number 9.

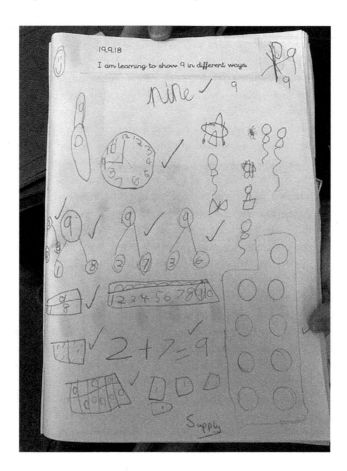

As you can see, representations have included part–part–whole models, a ruler, a 10s frame, a clock and Numicon. These were entirely the child's own choice.

The teachers in Year 1 have been very pleased with the responses of all the children.

The Year 1 teacher at Christ Church has also been making use of these slides. This is what she has said:

> I have found number work successful in my class. I have found that it has brought out conversations and questions from the children. They are now spotting right

angles on all sorts of things which is fantastic. It's introducing them to new language and is allowing them to see numbers in different ways giving them that level of mastery.

Of course, representing numbers in different ways does not stop in the Early Years and Year 1, children need the opportunity to do this throughout their schooling. Examples of how numbers are represented in Key Stage 2 are included in later sections of this book.

Connecting quantities to numbers and numerals

In January 2019, I was shown material that the National Centre for Excellence in the Teaching of Mathematics had provided for its Maths Hub Subject Knowledge Enhancement workgroup which I was privileged to be delivering for one of the London hubs. The material shared ideas from the research of Siemon et al.'s (2015) *Teaching Mathematics to Foundations and Middle Years* (2nd ed.). This research was concerned with how children can connect quantities to numbers and numerals. They suggested six possible connections:

1   A collection is presented to the children with manipulatives and in picture form. The children need to match the collection to the number word.

2   A collection is presented to the children with manipulatives and in picture form. The children need to match the collection to the numeral.

3   A number word is presented to the children, and they make and draw a collection.

4   A numeral is presented to the children, and they make and draw a collection.

5   Children can match a number word to its numeral.

6   Children can match a numeral to its word.

These suggestions are helpful and well worth considering. Consider some of the spellings of our number words – let alone English words, in general; spelling can become a real distraction for many children and can cause anxiety for some because words are not always spelt as they sound. Take counting: 1 sounds like *won*, 4 sounds like *for*, 8 sounds like *ate* – why on earth – or erth, would it be spelt *eight*? However, because this word looks so strange, it might be one children remember. The other numbers to 10 are usually less problematic. We want children to access all of these numerals and their written number equivalents. We also want them to access these without any anxiety.

I like the idea of a colour-coded approach, as I believe it initially helps some children. We use cards that are the same colour as the Numicon plates in words and numbers so that children have an initial clue, by the colour, and can be confident that they can match the numerals and words together. This makes a good pairs game, or the cards could be used as flashcards. The main idea is that the children become familiar with the written format of the number so that when they are ready, they can read the numbers in words without any clues. This is proving to be extremely helpful for many children.

Diagram 1.7

Following are a couple examples.

The following shows how some of the connections could be presented. My expectation would be that the children make a number, draw a picture of what they made, name the number and record it but only as these fit with the aforementioned connections.

1   A collection is presented to the children with manipulatives and in picture form. The children need to match the collection to the number word. Ensure the colour of the number word and the numeral match the appropriate Numicon plate.

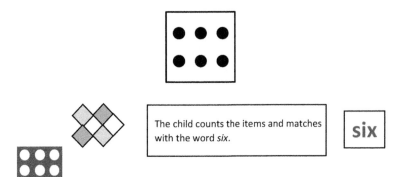

2   A collection is presented to the children with manipulatives and in picture form. The children need to match the collection to the symbol. Again, ensure the colour of the number word and the numeral match the appropriate Numicon plate.

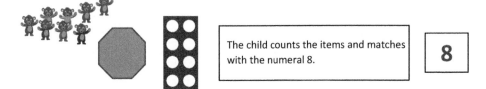

3   A number word is presented to the children, and they make and draw a collection. Provide the appropriate Numicon plate with matching coloured numeral and word.

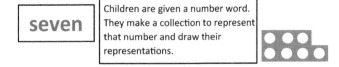

4   A symbol is presented to the children, and they make and draw a collection. Again, provide the appropriate Numicon plate and matching coloured word and numeral.

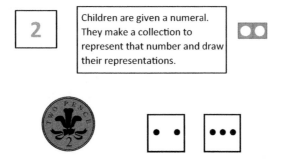

| 2 | Children are given a numeral. They make a collection to represent that number and draw their representations. |

5   Children can match a number word to its symbol. Make sure that the colours are the same.

five   5

6   Children can match a symbol to its word. Again, ensure that the colours are the same.

8   eight

I believe colour-coding is important initially as this is a way most children can successfully access activities such as these. Obviously, when the children are ready, they should be able to carry out these activities without the colour clues simply recognising the number words (maybe through the shapes they make) and numerals. Then, eventually, they will be able to recognise, read and spell the number words, as well as match them to the appropriate numerals.

Odd and even numbers

As part of their exploration of numbers, children discover odd and even numbers. Numicon is a great resource for this. They clearly show that an even number is made from pairs of two and that an odd number is made from pairs of two with an extra one. This is sometimes referred to as a 'sticky up bit' or 'the one without a friend'. To be mathematically correct, we need to tell the children that there is an extra one!

Diagram 1.8

Four is two pairs of two and so is even. Eight is four pairs of two and so is even.

Five is two pairs of two with one extra and so is odd.

Nine is four pairs of two with one extra and so is odd.

Encouraging children to count in 2s is helpful so that they can understand that an even number is always a multiple of 2 and that an odd number is always a multiple of 2 with an extra 1.

Gradually, children will develop the understanding that if an integer can be divided exactly by 2 then it is an even number. They will soon recognise that the last digit of an even number is 2, 4, 6, 8 or 0. For example, −36, 4 and 78 are all even numbers.

They will also develop the understanding that if an integer cannot be divided exactly by 2, then it is an odd number. They will recognise that the last digit of an odd number is 1, 3, 5, 7 or 9. For example, −13, 7 and 35 are all odd numbers.

Calling out different numbers, of various sizes, and asking children to, for example, clap once if it is an even number and clap twice if it is odd is fun. The children only need to consider the 1s number, so saying numbers such as 345, 23,678, 412,983 and 5,367,321 and stressing the 1s number are achievable and add excitement for young children. They do not need to know the composition of the numbers said by the teacher; they simply focus on the 1s number to know whether it is odd or even regardless of how many digits a number has.

In Year 1, children are expected to count in 2s, 5s and 10s. This opportunity is ideal for thinking about odd and even numbers and exploring the patterns made. For example, when we count in 2s and 10s, we are counting in even numbers. When counting in 5s, we alternate odd, even, odd and so on. Can the children explain why? If they have spent time exploring these numbers with Numicon, they should be able to! The notes and guidance section of the requirements for Number – number and place value in the national curriculum – suggest that counting in 2s, 5s and 10s from different multiples will help develop a child's recognition of patterns in the number system, such as odd and even numbers. This, of course, should continue in later years as the children continue to count in multiples of different sizes, including 25, 50, 75 and 100.

By the end of Key Stage 1, children should know that

- an even number is a number that can be divided into two equal groups.
- an odd number is a number that cannot be divided into two equal groups.

In addition to using Numicon, giving children small groups of counters or cubes and organising them into two equal groups is a good idea. Those that can be shared into two equal groups exactly are even; those that have one left over are odd.

In lower Key Stage 2, we should continue exploring odd and even numbers by, for example, sorting numbers into Carroll or Venn diagrams. Numbers could be sorted against two criteria, for example, even numbers and multiples of 5. From this, they can clearly see which are even numbers, multiples of 5, both even numbers and multiples of 5 or neither.

The following numbers can be sorted into both types of diagram: 18, 25, 36, 40, 55, 67, 72, 75, 135 and 199.

Carroll diagram

	Even numbers	Not even numbers
Multiples of 5	40	25 55 75 135
Not multiples of 5	18 36 72 84	199 67

Diagram 1.9

Venn diagram

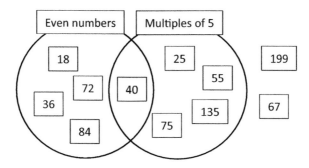

Venn and Carroll diagrams are no longer specified in the statistics section of the national curriculum. However, they are very useful tools for sorting different types of numbers and shapes into given criteria; they easily demonstrate what fits and what does not fit the criteria. We should therefore still use them.

In addition to sorting, we should also ask questions involving further investigation and reasoning; for example,

- I am an odd number.
- I am greater than 46 and less than 55.

■ My digit total is 8.

■ What number am I?

A digit total is the sum of the digits that make the number; for example, 363 has a digit total of nine: $3 + 6 + 3 = 18, 1 + 8 = 9$

Always, sometimes, never true?

■ Multiples of 7 are all odd.

■ Multiples of 4 are all even.

■ The sum of two odd numbers will always be even.

■ If I subtract an even number from an odd number, the difference could be either odd or even.

We could set similar statements for adding even numbers, three odd numbers and so on and similar for subtraction.

Activities such as 'always, sometimes, never' require children to develop a proof for their thinking with examples and, if there are any, counterexamples. Their 'proofs' will begin very simplistically, maybe by making lists of numbers that fit the given criteria. We should always expect them to be able to explain why; for example, adding two odd numbers will always give an even number. From their work in Key Stage 1, they should be able to explain that two odd numbers are two even numbers each with an extra one. These two extra ones make two, so the sum will be even.

Over time, we would expect their proof to become more mathematically sound and lead to generalisations.

For example, in upper Key Stage 2, we might ask children to prove that multiplying two odd numbers will always give an odd product. Again, children might begin by multiplying odd numbers together to create a list showing the products are odd, for example, $3 \times 5 = 15, 7 \times 9 = 63, 9 \times 11 = 99$. However, we would want them to refine this to deepen their understanding.

For example, we could say that we can represent any number as n. To ensure that it is even, we would multiply it by two to give the generalisation of $2n$. To ensure that it is an odd number, we would need to add one, to give $2n + 1$.

We can then begin to explore at greater depth, that an odd number multiplied by an odd number gives an odd product.

Diagram 1.10

This could be the first step:

Take the example 7×9; we can break 7 into $6 + 1$ (an even number add one) and 9 into $8 + 1$ (another even number add one). We can then multiply using a grid like this:

	6	1
8	48	8
1	6	1

If we add the numbers in the grid, we can see that $7 \times 9 = 62 + 1$. The add-1 proves that the product will always be odd. We can do this for any odd whole number multiplied by any other odd whole number. We can also adapt this idea for multiplying 2 or more even numbers and an even number by an odd number.

For example, when multiplying an even number by an odd number or vice versa, we can use the same idea presented earlier. Take 8×7; we can leave 8 as 8 because it is an even number and break 7 into $6 + 1$.

	6	1
8	48	8

There is no extra one, so the product is always even.

After this, the next step, that some children will be able to cope with is algebraic proof.

If we multiply an odd number by an odd number, we could make the statement $(2n + 1)(2n + 1)$. If we multiply the terms, we would get $4n^2 + 2n + 2n + 1$. Again, the add 1 is the proof we need that multiplying odd numbers gives an odd product.

Odd and even numbers are mentioned specifically in the requirements of the national curriculum in multiplication and division for Year 2. They are not mentioned again. However, these numbers provide opportunities for reasoning and problem solving in Key Stage 2 and should not be forgotten. These properties are part of number sense, such as prime numbers, square numbers and cube numbers, so we need to continue making connections with these numbers and the other areas of number sense in the curriculum. There is more on prime, square and cube numbers in later sections of this book.

Mathematical games

As part of my work with EYFS teachers, whether it be delivering courses or working alongside them in the classroom, one thing I always recommend is having a designated games table in an area of the classroom set up specifically for playing mathematical games.

Some time ago, I met a headteacher who had visited some schools in Singapore to investigate their education system, particularly their methodology for teaching mathematics. She told me that in some of the kindergarten settings she had visited, children spent a great deal of time playing games. Doing so apparently helped develop the children's reasoning skills. Well, I thought that was a great idea and worth copying back here in the UK! I encourage EYFS teachers to choose a simple game, for example, Snakes and Ladders, Shut the Box or dominoes, and spend a few sessions teaching it to a group of children. When these children are confident in playing the game, they then teach it to another group, and the next group teach a third and so on until the whole class can play it. We found that playing games certainly does help develop reasoning skills. Games also have the added bonus of improving social skills, for example, cooperation, turn taking, not always wanting to win and so on – not mention children's ability to subitise.

During the planning for mastery in the EYFS two-day training courses that I deliver, developing a designated games table is part of the teachers' gap task. On returning for day 2, the feedback has always been extremely positive, and the idea is one that they continue using. Children were able to play the games, take turns and be more socially aware of themselves and other children. A long time ago, playing games was something families did. Sadly, this is rarely the case these days. Television, iPads and other more isolated interests have taken over. I think we need to be aware of this and make sure that playing games is an integral part of our teaching throughout the key stages.

A couple years ago, I was teaching a group of Reception children to play dominoes. Dominoes were in the classroom for the children to choose to use if they wanted to. Out of the six in my group, none had chosen to use the dominoes, so these were new to most of them. One boy vaguely recalled seeing them at home and knew that they were used as a game but could not recall how it was played. The children started off by getting to know the dominoes, looking at the patterns made by the dots, identifying dominoes that had a total of, for example, six dots and sorting them according to different criteria. They then learned how to play the game. Five out of the six children were really enthusiastic. The sixth was not interested and went off to do something else. We needed a few more sessions for the children to become competent enough to teach others. The teacher I was working with followed this up, and she later reported that most of the class could now play the game and that many of them chose to play it during their child-initiated time. Similarly, in the nursery classes at the same school, the teachers followed the same procedure to teach the children how to play skittles in the outside area and expected the children to record their results using Numicon plates and then their own mark making. This worked well (it did take a lot of time and patience on the teachers' part!), but it was successful, and again, many children chose to play the game with their friends recording their results in their own time.

Once one game has been taught and most of the class are able to play, another game can be introduced. What begins as a guided activity then becomes a child-initiated activity which is purposeful and enjoyable for many children. Over time, a selection of the games learned are left out in a games area and children play them. This is more successful than simply having a selection of games that the children do not know how to play left in the classroom on the off-chance children might find them somewhere and have a go at playing them without knowing how.

Charlotte Cameron, a Reception teacher at St Mary's Church of England School, Chessington, has been trying out this idea. She has given this feedback:

> The introduction of games into our continuous provision has been an overwhelming success. As practitioners we teach one group of children how to play a game and they teach their friends as well as adults that come into our classroom. The children have access to a wide range of games that are stored together on an open shelf in the classroom and they are always in constant use. The games have

given them a much deeper understanding of mathematical concepts especially number and create an environment where children are not frightened to give it a go and support one another. It has also encouraged sharing and turn taking as well developing their language skills. We look forward to expanding our game provision to continue the impact already seen.

References

Bobis, J, *Early spatial thinking and the development of Number Sense*, Institute of Education Sciences, 1996, http://opentolearning.weebly.com/what-is-number-sense.html.

Gelman, R & Gallistell, CR, *The child's understanding of number*, Harvard University Press, Cambridge, MA, 1978.

Gifford, S, Back, J, & Griffiths, R, *Making numbers: Using manipulatives to teach arithmetic*, Oxford University Press, Oxford, 2016.

Numicon (published by Oxford University Press) www.oxfordprimary.co.uk/numicon, Oxford, England.

Piaget, J, *Origins of intelligence in the child*. Routledge & Kegan Paul, London, 1936.

Siemon, D, *Assessment for common misunderstandings: Introducing the big ideas*, University of the Free State, Bloemfontein, South Africa, 2006.

Recommended books for further reading

Gifford, S, Back, J, & Griffiths, R, *Making numbers: Using manipulatives to teach arithmetic*, Oxford University Press, Oxford, 2016.

Siemon, D, et al., *Teaching mathematics to foundations and middle years*, 2nd edn, Oxford University Press, Australia, 2015.

2

Numerical reasoning

This section includes:

- Variation
- Place value
- Comparing, ordering and rounding
- Suggested progression for teaching place value
- Fractions: what is a fraction?
- Part–whole model for fractions
- Quotient model for fractions
- Fractions as numbers
- Fractions as operators
- Fractions of quantities
- Fractions of shape
- Equivalence
- Improper fractions and mixed numbers
- Calculating with fractions
- Decimals
- Percentages
- Linking fractions, decimals and percentages
- Ratio and proportion
- Solving fraction-related problems
- Fractions and percentages with pie charts
- Suggested progression for teaching fractions

Introduction

Numerical reasoning

In 2010, Estyn (The Education and Training Inspectorate for Wales) defined *numeracy* as 'the ability to apply simple numerical facts, skills and reasoning to real-life problems. Procedural knowledge focuses on the ability to recall numerical facts and procedures. Numerical reasoning focuses on the ability to apply those facts and procedures within a wide range of contexts'.

Numerical reasoning is about 'making sense' of the mathematics we encounter. It requires active engagement from the learner to think mathematically, choosing what to do and how to do it. Numerical reasoning involves place value and all things related to fractions: decimals, percentages, ratio and proportion and much more. In fact, I would argue that numerical reasoning is involved in most areas of mathematics. In this section, we focus specifically on place value and fractions related concepts.

Variation

Before beginning this section on numerical reasoning, it is worth spending a little time exploring variation because this will be a feature of many of the areas covered in this book. Variation is an important aspect of teaching that we have overlooked for many decades.

Variation is not new. Dienes talked about it in the 1970s, and before him, people such as Festinger in the 1950s, who said that variation is 'the art of sequencing similar but increasingly complex problems to generate disturbance of some sort for the learner' (Festinger 1957). Unfortunately, in this country as in many others in the Western world, we did little with variation until recently. The Chinese have been implementing this idea since the late 1970s to improve the teaching and learning of mathematics in their country. Since paying particular attention to variation, Chinese teachers' teaching and children's mastery of mathematics have improved massively.

Gu suggested that variation is used

> to illustrate essential features of a concept by demonstrating various visual materials and instances, or to highlight essential characteristics of a concept by varying non-essential features. The goal of using variation is to help students understand the essential features of a concept by differentiating them from non-essential features and further develop a scientific concept.
>
> (1999, p. 186)

In 1963, Gattegno referred to variation in this way: 'All I must do is to present them with a situation so elementary that they all master it from the outset, and so fertile that they will all find a great deal to get out of it.'

The value of variation is so obvious that it surprises me how, in this country, we have never made effective use of it until recently. It also surprises me how we have not followed up on many other things that the wise men of mathematics from the US and Europe told us in the 1950s, 1960s and 1970s. Now, decades later, after our investigations into what makes good teaching in countries such as Singapore and China, we are starting to take notice of them. These mathematicians told us a few things that we should employ in order to help children achieve mastery in mathematics. For example, Bruner talked about using a concrete, pictorial and abstract approach in our teaching. He said that children need a mixture of all three throughout their education. In the past, we often gave children manipulatives (concrete) in the Early Years Foundation Stage (EYFS) and Key Stage 1 but only gave them to children who were struggling in Key Stage 2. In Key Stage 2, we tended to focus on the abstract. Richard Skemp said that conceptual and procedural understanding should go together; children need both. In the past, we often went too quickly into the teaching of procedures without helping the children to understand how and why they work. David Ausubel suggested that we use what we already know and build on that. Activities, such as giving the children a fact and asking them to make up others from it, are useful for developing flexible thinkers. Lev Vygotsky said that we learn best by talking to each other. Nowadays, opportunities for paired and group talk are given, which is great. In my early days of teaching, a silent classroom was considered a working classroom!

Variation is used in lesson design. Examples are carefully planned so that the main theme of the lesson is varied slightly and the children are encouraged to notice patterns and be able to discuss what is the same and what is different about the well-thought-out examples givens. There is a logical step-by-step approach in which children focus on what they have done and what they will do next. Examples and non-examples of concepts are included so that the children can explain what is the same, what is different and why to reinforce deep conceptual understanding.

The best part of variation is that it is about depth, not complexity. It is about simplicity to develop understanding for all children.

There are two main types of variation – conceptual and procedural – which can very simply be described as follows (Gu et al. 2004).

Conceptual variation

Same problem but varying the representation.

■ For example, 'Show me 36 using as many different representations as you can.' Representations can include anything, provided the children can explain their thinking about those they use. These could include Dienes, place-value counters, Gattegno charts, partitioning cards, double-sided counters, cubes, a 100 square and so on.

■ Showing examples and non-examples is also important; for example, 'This is 36 because . . . This is not 36 because . . .'.

Procedural variation

■ Vary the conditions, results and generalities:
  ○ Use the same problem but vary the numbers within the problem.
  ○ Use the same problem but vary the unknowns or the question being asked.
  ○ Use the same structure and numbers but vary the context, which might include aspects of measurement.

For example, take this problem: Freddie scored 245 points in the competition. Bertie scored 136 points more. How many points did Bertie score?

Varying the numbers:

Freddie scored 345, 445, 545, 645, . . . points in the competition. Bertie scored 136 points more. How many points did Bertie score?

Freddie scored 245 points in the competition. Bertie scored 236, 336, 436, 536, . . . points more. How many points did Bertie score?

It is important to ask the children what is the same and what is different about the problem and to question them on whether they need to complete another calculation or whether can they use what they already know.

Varying the unknown:

The problem could be varied by altering the question:

O Freddie scored 245 points in the competition. Bertie scored 381 points. How many more points did Bertie score?

O Freddie and Bertie scored 626 in a competition. Bertie scored 381 points. How many points did Freddie score?

When changing the question in these ways, again, asking the children to explain what is the same about the problem and what is different is important.

Varying the context:

Freddie spent £245 on a bike. Bertie spent £136 more. How much did Bertie pay for his bike?

■ Vary the method to solve the problem; for example, 'If I can add these two numbers together using a written method to find the solution, how else can I add the numbers together? Is there another way? And another . . .?'

■ Vary the application of the method; for example, 'I can use this method to subtract two numbers. How can I use this method to subtract numbers with decimal places, money, or length? Is the process the same?'

As previously mentioned, variation is explored as appropriate within the different sections of this book. Hopefully, this will enable you to gain a deeper understanding of this if you are new to variation.

Place value

Once children have mastered the numbers to 10 as discussed in the Number Sense section, it is time for them to begin developing a deep understanding of place value. Place value is a vital part of numerical reasoning and is an essential concept that the children need to master to be able to develop further mathematical understanding.

If children cannot count to 10 and master the counting principles discussed previously, they will not be able to progress on their mathematical journey. It is the same with place value. Place value is important in the general understanding of number and in its application to the four operations, both using mental calculation strategies and written methods as well as in the real-life application of measurement and statistics. If they have not mastered this key concept, their mathematical progress will be hindered, if not halted altogether.

After 9 comes 10, which is a new concept for the children in EYFS. Up to 9, children are dealing with 1s numbers. With numbers greater than 9, children now experience 10s and 1s. They need to move on from seeing 10 as ten 1s to seeing it as one 10 or a unit of 10, eleven 1s as one unit of 10 and one unit of 1, 12 as one unit of 10 and two units of one and so on. We need to give children very practical experiences for them to begin developing their understanding of this.

There are many ways in which we can do this, and we need to show the children a variety of them. One element of conceptual variation is to represent numbers in many ways.

Dienes equipment is one of the best resources to show children how 1s and 10s link together. Begin by asking children to make a group of ten 1s cubes. They then line these up alongside a 10 stick so that they can see that ten 1s is equivalent to one unit of 10, 11 would be one 10 stick and one cube, 12 would be one 10 stick and two cubes and so on.

Diagram 2.1

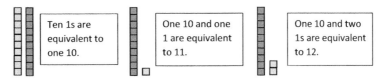

Bundling straws is also a good way to show children how 10s and 1s are made up for example.

Diagram 2.2

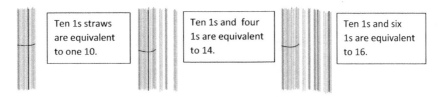

Making towers of 10 interlocking cubes and adding extra ones to make 10s and 1s numbers work just as well.

Diagram 2.3

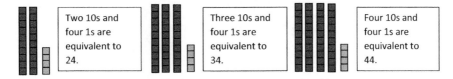

We need to be mindful of the fact that the children have worked on numbers to 20 in Year R, and so some may be able to work with greater two-digit numbers for place value than specified in the national curriculum.

Place-value charts are really helpful as a visual resource to go with Dienes, straws and cubes.

Diagram 2.4

10	1
2	3

In Year 1, children could make the number using practical resources and then show this using digit cards in a place-value grid similar to the one shown earlier. I prefer using the numbers as headings rather than the initials *t* and *o* because the actual numbers make it more obvious. Also *o* can be confused with zero. As children progress through Year 1, I would ask them to make numbers to 99. I also expected them to build the numbers using practical equipment, draw a picture of what they make and write a number statement. 'Make it, draw it, say it and write it' is a mantra for me these days!

At one school, teachers were linking tens and ones to money. Some children were able to tell their teachers that there were 100 pence in £1, so they thought they would challenge these children to use money to explore 100s, 10s and 1s. The children were very successful.

The following is an example of one child's results.

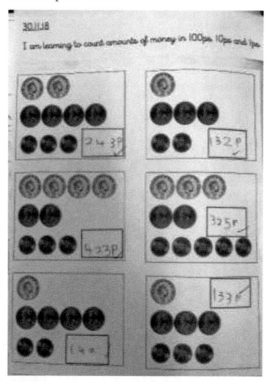

In Year 2, I would encourage children to make three-digit numbers because they have had experienced two-digit numbers since Year R. I would only do this for place value, not for addition and subtraction.

Diagram 2.5

100	10	1
1	2	3

Again, I would encourage them to make the number, draw a picture of it, talk about what they have done and then write a number statement, such as 100 + 20 + 3 = 123.

Ross (2002) talks about four different elements of place value:

■ Positional

■ Multiplicative

■ Additive

■ Base 10

These elements are crucial in helping children develop a depth of understanding of this important concept of mathematics. I think we should be using these terms with the children at the beginning of Key Stage 2.

Let's use the number 2586 as an example:

■ Positional place value is where the digit is positioned. The 2 is positioned in the thousands position, the 5 is in the hundreds, the 8 in the tens and the 6 in the ones.

■ Multiplicative place value is when the digit is multiplied by the position it is in to give its true value. The 2 is multiplied by 1000 to give its value of 2000, the 5 is multiplied by 100 to give its value of 500, the 8 is multiplied by 10 to give its value of 80 and the 6 is multiplied by 1 to give its value of 6.

■ Additive place value is when the different values are added together to give the whole number: 2000 + 500 + 80 + 6 = 2586.

Currently, in many schools, the focus of place value concentrates on the additional element rather than the positional and multiplicative elements.

From my experience working with schools, not enough time is spent on these fundamental aspects. From looking at books and observing teaching, I have seen many teachers move too quickly into the additive aspect of place value, where children partition, for example, 365 into 300 + 60 + 5. They may also give the children digits to organise to make different numbers. They then move on to comparing and ordering. For a depth of understanding, children need to really understand the positional and multiplicative aspects of place value first.

Base 10 indicates that our number system increases and decreases by powers of 10. So, when we multiply 47 by 10, each digit becomes 10 times greater, giving 470. When we divide by 10. each digit becomes 10 times smaller, so 47 divided by 10 would give 4.7. We are, in effect, scaling the numbers up and down by powers of 10.

The zero at the end of 470 is the placeholder. We must never refer to adding and taking away zeroes when we multiply and divide by powers of 10. A lot of children do say this! I was keen to discover why this might be. So, a few years ago, I investigated in a Year 2 class. I asked the children what they would do to multiply 4 by 10. They all said add a zero. I repeated this in Year 1 with the same results. Then I went into the Reception class to look at its provision for mathematics and saw a washing line with the 10s numbers hanging from it. That got me thinking that four-year-olds would recognise the 4 of 40 because that number is important to them due to being four years old and that they might perceive 40 as 4 with a zero on the end. I do not know if I am right, but it does make a certain amount of sense. That means that EYFS teachers need to explicitly talk about 40 being four groups of 10s and that there are no ones, so zero must be placed in the 1s position. If we can pre-empt misconceptions arising, it will make children's learning and our teaching more successful.

If they develop this misconception, they are likely to keep it, and it will be hard work to eradicate in later years. Adding zeroes does not work for decimal numbers. If we simply add zero to 4.7 when we multiply by 10, we end up with 4.70, exactly the same number. I have seen examples of children doing this in Years 5 and 6.

In the national curriculum section for fractions, in Year 3 children need to 'count up and down in tenths and recognise that tenths arise from dividing an object into 10 equal parts and in dividing one-digit numbers or quantities by 10'. I believe that the children need to understand that tenths are part of place value, and this should be included in the number and place-value sections, as well as the fractions section, of the curriculum.

1000	100	10	1	.	$\frac{1}{10}$
2	3	1	6	.	

In the work that we have been doing with Year 3, we use place-value charts as shown with digit cards and cubes or counters where one colour represents one particular value. We begin with four-digit whole numbers because they are familiar with three-digit numbers from Years 2. An extra place is not difficult for children to understand. Of course, this is just for place value, not addition and subtraction.

We work through Ross's (2002) positional, multiplicative and additive aspects of these numbers using the correct terminology. We then work on the base 10 aspect of place value by multiplying and dividing numbers by 10 using one- and two-digit numbers.

1000	100	10	1	.	$\frac{1}{10}$
		1	6	.	7

Because the children know the positional, multiplicative and additive aspects of place value, they know that 7 is in the tenths position and so must be multiplied by 1 tenth. They do this by repeated addition and so know that the value of this digit is 7 tenths. We then discuss that 16 and $\frac{7}{10}$ is equivalent to 16.7. A lesson is spent converting between fractions and decimals in this way, and it seems to make perfect sense to most children, especially as many have seen decimal numbers before in real life. This is an example of one child's work linking whole numbers and tenths to their decimal notation.

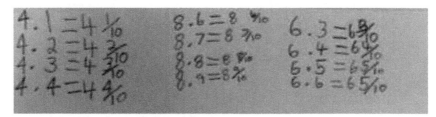

As part of practice and application, we then ask the children to measure in centimetres and millimetres. They, first, look at their rulers and explore the divisions on them, identifying the centimetre and then millimetre divisions. They practise drawing lines of different centimetre and millimetre lengths. After they are confident doing this, they are given different lengths of paper to measure and record in centimetres and millimetres and centimetres using decimal notation, for example, 12 cm 3 mm = 12.3 cm. They then draw, measure and record their own lines. This has been very successful.

This example shows how the children have been measuring lines and connecting decimal notation for centimetres with centimetres and millimetres.

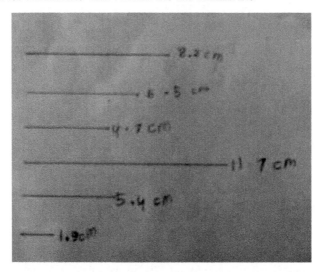

We have delivered a similar series of lessons in Year 4. Children are introduced to hundredths in the fractions section of the national curriculum. Again, we should be introducing these when we teach place value; for example, a 6 positioned in the hundredths position is multiplied by 1 hundredth to give 6 hundredths. We can then explore the two equivalent ways of expressing this, for example, $18.76 = 18$ and $\frac{76}{100}$.

1000	100	10	1	.	$\frac{1}{10}$	$\frac{1}{100}$
2	3	1	8	.	7	6

As with Year 3, children were given practice tasks that involve length, focusing on metres and centimetres. They measured lengths of string or distances in the classroom and playground and then linked them to notation, such as 3 m 65 cm = 365 cm = 3.65 m.

The following is an example of this from a Year 4 child at Georgian Gardens.

Hundredths link so well with percentages. Percentages are a topic for Year 5, but they could be introduced in Year 4. I have worked with several Year 4 classes exploring tenths and hundredths. We looked at food packaging. The children identified and wrote down the different numbers that they see. Usually these involve tenths, hundredths and percentages. On one occasion, a boy found 17%, so we talked about where percentages can be found. Most could tell me that they see them in shops during sale times, food packaging, phones and iPads. We talked about their phones and iPads, and the children knew that if their iPad is showing 17%, they would need to charge it soon and that it would show 100% when it was fully charged. We do not do any real work on percentages but do link them to hundredths to familiarise them with this concept, which they actually have a basic understanding of from their experiences outside school. Their task was to write different percentages as decimals and hundredths, reducing the fractions to their simplest form if they could.

The following is an example of the work children carry out in Year 4 linking percentages and hundredths.

11% = 0.11
8% = 0.08
10% = 0.10
7% = 0.07
30% = 0.30
3% = 0.03
17% = 0.17
4% = 0.04
70% = 0.70
44% = 0.44
80% = 0.80
2% = 0.02
2.5%
1% = 0.01
0% = 0
6% = 0.06
24% = 0.24
15% = 0.15
13% = 0.13
18% = 0.18
50% = 0.50
99% = 0.99
46% = 0.46
100% = 1.00
5% = 0.05

I also thought I would try out this problem with the children: A coat was reduced in a sale by 20%. It now costs £80. What was the original price of the coat? They set the problem out using double-sided counters, with each counter represented 20%.

Interestingly, because the children could count in 20s, they could easily work out that they needed five counters to represent 100%.

Diagram 2.6

From this model the fact that each counter was worth £20 was really obvious, so the reduction must be £20 and the original price was £100. Most of the class got the correct answer straight away! I gave them a few to practise independently by varying the cost of the coat and, for some, the percentage reduction. Visual representations and manipulatives make such a huge difference in how children can perceive problems.

The bar model is a key visual representation that schools are beginning to embed. The coat problem could be drawn using this bar model, which is mentioned at the end of this section when solving problems related to fractions is looked at. Bar modelling is considered in more depth in the section on additive reasoning.

Diagram 2.7

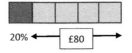

The expectation for children in Year 5 is that, in fractions, they explore thousandths. In the same way shown earlier, this is part of place value, so it should be covered then. The 5 is in the thousandths position, so it is multiplied by 1 thousandth to give 5 thousandths.

1000	100	10	1	.	$\frac{1}{10}$	$\frac{1}{100}$	$\frac{1}{1000}$
2	3	1	8	.	7	6	5

To practise, children convert single–digit numbers with three decimal places to their equivalent fraction. For example, $8.765 = 8\frac{765}{1000}$.

They then go on to apply this to measuring capacities and volumes or different masses and record these in different ways, for example, 3525 ml = 3 l. 525 ml = 3.525 l.

Here is an example of some work that Year 5 carried out. They measured different volumes and then recorded them in litre and millilitre, millilitre and litre formats.

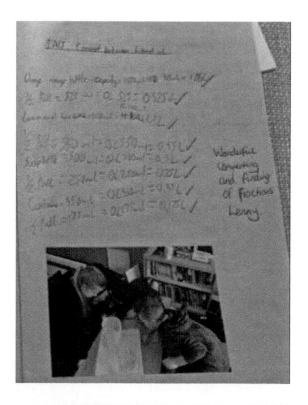

Comparing, ordering and rounding

When the children have a deep understanding of place value, they can begin to compare numbers and then order and round them. The children begin by comparing pairs of numbers. They should use the greater than, less than and equal to symbols that we considered in the Number Sense section of the book. They should be comparing numbers of a suitable size that match with the place-value work they have been covering.

Here is an example of comparing money from a Year 1 class.

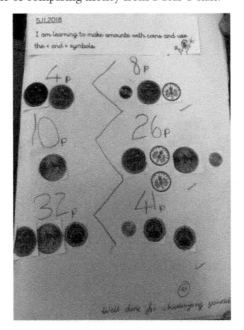

The following example shows how Year 1 children have been working on using a ruler to draw accurate lines. Once they had drawn their lines, they had to compare the shortest and longest and find the difference between the two.

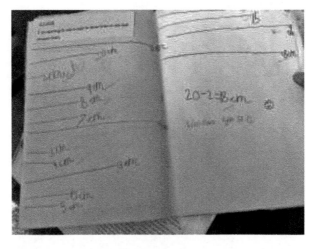

Numbers with decimals places should be included as numbers in their own right and within the context of measurement. For example, in Years 3 and 4, we asked the children to compare pairs of different lengths and then make them equal.

$$4.6 \text{ cm} > 2.1 \text{ cm}, 2.1 \text{ cm} < 4.6 \text{ cm}, 2.1 \text{ cm} = 4.6 \text{ cm} - 2.5 \text{ cm}, 4.6 \text{ cm} = 2.1 \text{ cm} + 2.5 \text{ cm}.$$

Here is an example of some work carried out on this in Year 4.

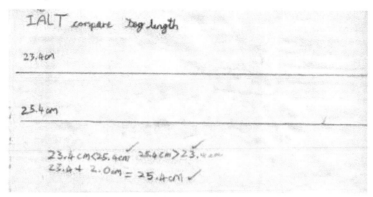

The lengths were accurately drawn; we had to crop the photograph!

After children have explored comparing two numbers, they begin to order three and then four or more numbers. Again, the size of the numbers should reflect the place value work and, as appropriate, numbers with decimal places within context.

In Years 5 and 6, children work with numbers to 1 million and 10 million. One activity that they really enjoy is to build large numbers using interlocking cubes. We give the colours different values; for example, white cubes have a value of 1 million, blue have a value of 100,000, yellow have a value of 10,000 and so on until 1s, which might be orange. They record their numbers, and then we switch the values, so, for example, green cubes now have a value of 1 million and white have a value of 1. They compare their two numbers.

The following are some photographs of Year 5's work on this. Seeing the entirely different ways the three children recorded what they did is interesting. The examples are from children of different attainment levels.

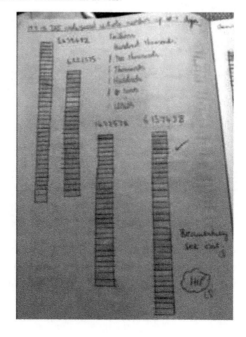

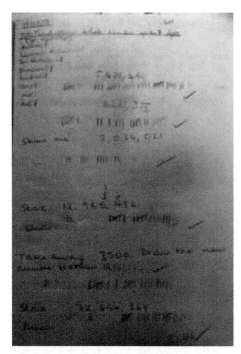

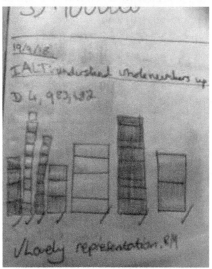

After ordering comes rounding. Rounding is a process that makes a number simpler to use but keeps its value close to the original. The result is less accurate, but rounded numbers are easier to use. For example, 267 is closer to 270 than 260. It is also closer to 300 than 200. 123 is closer to 120 than 130. It is also closer to 100 than 200. If we were to add 267 and 123, we could estimate the answer at about 390 or 400. As previously, work with the types of numbers used in place value.

In Key Stage 1, children could begin to round two-digit numbers to the nearest 10. They would need to use number lines so that they can visually see which 10 a number is closest to.

Diagram 2.8

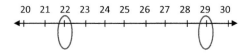

22 is closer to 20 than 30, so it would be rounded to 20.
29 is closer to 30 than 20, so it would be rounded to 30.

Twenty-five is not closer to either 20 or 30 but is rounded up to 30. The convention of rounding up for numbers ending with 5 has been used for decades. This applies to any number if a 5 is followed by zeros; for example, if we round 1445 to the nearest 10, it will be rounded to 1450. Now there is a 5 in the 10s, so this number would be rounded to 1500. Now there is a 5 in the 100s, so it would be rounded to 2000.

Various reasons for rounding up numbers that end with 5 have been suggested over the years. Possibly the simplest explanation that I have seen refers to the 10 digits we use. The first five digits are 0, 1, 2, 3 and 4, the other five are 5, 6, 7, 8 and 9. We round the first half down and the second half up, so numbers ending with five are rounded up.

- To round 25 to the nearest 10, 25 ends with 5 and therefore is rounded up.
- To round 250 to the nearest 10, the number ends with zero and so is rounded down. If rounding to the nearest 100, 250 ends with 50 and so must be rounded up.
- To round 2500 to the nearest 10 and 100 the number ends with zeros and so is rounded down. If rounding to the nearest 1000, 2500 ends with 500 and so must be rounded up.

And so it goes on!

I do think children need an explanation of why we round five up when they begin learning about rounding single and two-digit numbers, not just to be told that this is the rule, and this explanation seems plausible.

As they get older the numbers the children round become greater and numbers with decimal places are rounded to the nearest 1, 10th and 100th. They still benefit from using number lines as a visual representation.

Diagram 2.9

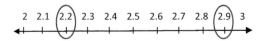

2.2 is closer to 2 than 3, so it would be rounded to 2.
2.9 is closer to 3 than 2, so it would be rounded to 3.

Suggested progression for teaching place value

This table sums up a suggested progression in place value that we are working on in some schools. I hope that you will find it helpful.

Year R	**Number sense:** count to at least 10 and know all there is to know about numbers to 10 in different everyday contexts; begin to know all number pairs for all numbers to 10; count in units of quantities to 10, e.g. hours, metres, hundreds, thousands; begin counting in multiples of 10, 5, 2 **Place value:** understand the place value of numbers from 11–20, knowing they are made up from units of ten and units of one
Year 1	**Number sense:** consolidate all there is to know about numbers to 10 in different everyday contexts; consolidate all number pairs for all numbers to 10; count beyond 10 in units of quantities to 10, e.g. hours, metres, millions; count in multiples of 10 to 120, 5 to 60 and 2 to 24; begin to work on multiplication facts for 10, 5 and 2; count in halves **Place value:** consolidate the place value of numbers from 11–20; increase place value for numbers to 50 and then 100; develop understanding of positional, multiplicative and additive place value; compare and order numbers looked at within place value; link to money (10 pence and 1 pence coins) and centimetre measurements
Year 2	**Number sense:** recap all previous work on counting; continue to learn multiplication and associated division facts for 10, 5 and 2; count in multiples of 4 (double 2) and 3; count in halves, thirds and fourths **Place value:** consolidate the place value of numbers to 100; increase place value to three-digit numbers; continue to develop understanding of positional, multiplicative and additive place value; compare and order numbers looked at within place value; link to money (£1, 10 pence and 1 pence coins) and centimetre measurements
Year 3	**Number sense:** recap all previous work on counting; begin to learn multiplication and associated division facts for 3 and 4; count in multiples of 8 (double 4), 6 (double 3) and 12 (double 6); begin these tables facts ensuring commutative facts are highlighted; count in tenths and other fractions **Place value:** consolidate the place value of numbers to 100; increase place value to four-digit numbers and tenths; multiply and divide numbers by 10; continue to develop understanding of positional, multiplicative and additive place value, introduce this terminology, include base 10; compare, order and round numbers looked at within place value; link to money (whole pounds and convert to pence) and centimetre and millimetre lengths
Year 4	**Number sense:** recap all previous work on counting; consolidate multiplication and associated division facts for 3, 6, 12, 4 and 8; count in multiples of 7, 9 and 11 and begin these tables facts ensuring commutative facts are highlighted; count in tenths and hundredths and other fractions **Place value:** consolidate the place value of four-digit numbers and tenths; introduce hundredths; multiply and divide numbers by 10 and 100; continue to develop understanding of positional, multiplicative, additive and base 10 place value using this terminology; compare, order and round numbers looked at within place value; link to money (whole pounds and convert to pence) and metre and centimetre lengths; link hundredths to percentages

Year 5	**Number sense:** rehearse all multiplication facts and associated division facts to 12 × 12; count in hundredths and thousandths and other fractions **Place value:** consolidate the place value of four-digit numbers with tenths and hundredths; introduce thousandths; extend place value of whole numbers to 1 million; multiply and divide numbers by 10, 100 and 1000; continue developing understanding of positional, multiplicative, additive and base 10 place value using this terminology; compare, order and round numbers looked at within place value; link to measurement (mass, capacity, volume, distance); continue to link hundredths to percentages
Year 6	**Number sense:** rehearse all multiplication facts and associated division facts to 12 × 12; count in tenths, hundredths and thousandths and other fractions; make links between fractions, decimals and percentages, converting from one to the others **Place value:** consolidate the place value for five-, six-digit numbers with up to three decimal places; explore numbers beyond 1 million; compare, order and round numbers looked at within place value; link to measurement (mass, capacity, volume, distance); continue to link hundredths to percentages and decimals

Fractions

If children are to master fractions and gain a deeper understanding of them, we need to invest more teaching time to allow for exploration, clarification, practice and application. I know Year 1 teachers who admit to spending only one or, at the most, two weeks on this concept. I would suggest that they need to spend at least four weeks to enable the children in this year group to gain a deep understanding of what a fraction is that can be built on in future years. The many Year 1 teachers I have worked with agree and are adapting their planning accordingly. Other year groups need at least six weeks over the course of a year. The best way to introduce the children to fractions is through problem solving. NRICH (https://nrich.maths. org/2361) provides a lovely Year R activity called 'Fair Feast' in which the children explore sharing a picnic between two imaginary children, although they could be sharing between two children in the class. The picnic involves a pizza cut into four pieces, two cartons of drink, eight tomatoes, four muffins and an apple. In this activity, children are sharing different quantities of different items. This could be extended to ask what would happen if a third child joined them for the picnic.

What is a fraction?

The most important thing about fractions is that they express a relationship. In his article 'How to Teach Fractions in KS1', Mike Askew beautifully describes this:

Take the idea of a quarter, I can use this to think about:

- The quarter of my cake I'm trying not to eat.
- How I'm a quarter of the way through the assignments I'm marking.
- That I like salad dressing to be one tablespoon of vinegar to three tablespoons of oil. So if I want to make a large jar, a quarter of it needs to be vinegar.
- How the shrub I planted is about a quarter of the height to which it will grow, according to its label

I could go on. The thing to note is that, tempting cake aside, a 'quarter' in these examples does not stand for a 'thing'; it expresses a relationship. You don't need to know how many assignments, how much dressing I need or what type of shrub I planted, but you can make sense of a 'quarter' each time.

Fractions are tools for thinking about and describing relationships: they are not things or objects.

Except, unfortunately, in primary school.

(2014)

That children understand that a fraction represents an equal part of a whole is so important. We need to teach this explicitly and spend as much time as necessary helping children understand this. The whole can be discrete, where a set of items makes the whole, for example, a pile of marbles. It can be continuous, where the whole is one item, for example, a length of string. It can be definite where the size is known, for example, 12 marbles. It can be indefinite, where the parts are known but the whole is not, for example, a third of a piece of string which is equivalent to 10 cm.

When introducing writing a fraction to younger children, we should draw the vinculum first to show we are breaking a whole into parts. Then we write the denominator to show how many parts there are and, finally, the numerator to show how many parts we are considering. The word *vinculum* is the name of the line. In Latin, it means 'to bond together', which is just what it does — bonds together the numerator and the denominator!

$$\frac{1}{3} \quad \begin{matrix} \text{numerator} \\ \text{vinculum} \\ \text{denominator} \end{matrix}$$

Part–whole model for fractions

The first concept in fractions that the children need to know about is that fractions are equal parts of a whole. A few years ago, I watched a teacher from Shanghai teaching children about parts and wholes. She began with a map of China and talked about that being the whole and the different cities and regions being the parts. I thought that was a great idea and adapted it to show the UK and the four parts: England, Scotland, Wales and Northern Ireland. Spending some time discussing wholes and unequal parts first made a lot of sense. So, we do that with lots of different things that children are familiar with, for example, the classroom, their bedroom, a farm or park, skeleton, dinosaur – anything really. When they can identify the whole and different unequal parts. Then we move onto looking at equal parts, and that is where our fractions begin.

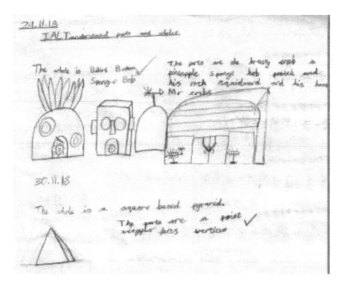

This example is of work carried out on unequal parts and wholes in Year 3 and 4 at Georgian Gardens.

This is a Year 3's idea from Christ Church Primary School. The whole is the classroom, and the unequal wholes are different elements of the classroom.

From Year 1, we need to show children visual representations of equal parts, for example, using the bar model.

Diagram 2.10

Children can model this concept using, for example, strips of paper, interlocking cubes and double-sided counters to represent their own fractions.

Diagram 2.11

In this example, the whole has five equal parts; each part is $\frac{1}{5}$. $\frac{2}{5}$ are red, and $\frac{3}{5}$ are yellow. Therefore, $\frac{2}{5} + \frac{3}{5} = \frac{5}{5}$, or one whole. We need to encourage children to consider commutativity and inverse. If they know $\frac{2}{5} + \frac{3}{5} = 1$, they also know that $\frac{3}{5} + \frac{2}{5} = 1$ because addition is commutative. They also know that $1 - \frac{2}{5} = \frac{3}{5}$ and $1 - \frac{3}{5} = \frac{2}{5}$ because subtraction is the inverse of addition.

In this country, I think we make the mistake of focusing the children on halves and fourths or quarters in Year 1 instead of focusing on what a fraction actually is. If they really understand that a fraction is an equal part of a whole, how many parts there are does not matter. In Singapore, when they begin fractions, they have a variety of parts.

As part of variation, we should show different examples and non-examples and ask the children what is the same and what is different about them. The following is an example.

Diagram 2.12

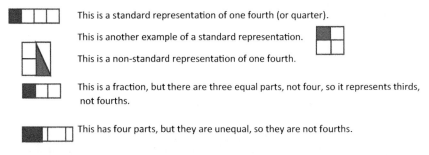

This is a standard representation of one fourth (or quarter).

This is another example of a standard representation.

This is a non-standard representation of one fourth.

This is a fraction, but there are three equal parts, not four, so it represents thirds, not fourths.

This has four parts, but they are unequal, so they are not fourths.

We need to explore simple equivalence from Year R. We often teach equivalent fractions as if they are a new topic when, actually, they should be included right from the beginning.

In the EYFS, children are often asked to make half a turn; if they are then asked to make the other half turn, they have made one whole turn and so can begin to link that one half added to another half equals one whole and therefore two halves are equivalent to one whole. They also start sharing in EYFS, so linking sharing to fractions makes perfect sense; for example, if we share four grapes between two children, each child will have two grapes, which is half of the whole amount. If we put the two parts together, we will have the whole amount again. If we share nine grapes between three children, each child will have three, which is one third, two have two thirds, which is six. If we put the three parts together, we will have the whole again. As a teacher, demonstrating how to write a fraction using the correct vocabulary and notation is helpful so that the children become familiar with how fractions appear and the vocabulary associated with them. Some may want to try writing them; others will not.

The National Centre for Excellence in the Teaching of Mathematics (NCETM) have a great physical resource for equivalence which I have used in Years 1 and 2.

Diagram 2.13

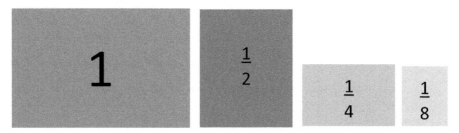

By placing two halves on top of the one whole card, children can clearly see that two halves are equivalent to one whole. Repeating this for fourths and eighths enables children to make the generalisation that the numerator and the denominator need to be the same to make one whole. They should then be able to tell you other equivalences to one whole, for example, three thirds, six sixths. They can also explore other equivalences using the cards; for example, two fourths and four eighths are equivalent to one half. They can see that one half is half of one whole, one fourth is half of one half and one eighth is half of one fourth. Using this resource, children begin to understand that one eighth of the same whole is the smallest fraction and so recognise that the larger the denominator, the smaller the fraction. Too many children have the misconception that half is smaller than, for example, one eighth because two is smaller than eight.

I have sets of cards that I give to Year 2 children to explore. The following are some examples.

Diagram 2.14

The first thing the children do is talk to their partner about what they see on the cards. Most of them can identify the number of parts each shape has been divided into and how many parts are coloured and how many are not. They can make the link between fourths and eighths and also sixths and thirds. Calling quarters fourths as well as quarters makes sense because in fourths you can hear four and so know that there are four parts. They can see from the cards that, for example, six eighths are equivalent to three fourths, four sixths of one circle are shaded and two sixths are not. They then sort them into groups according to their own criteria. Some sort according to the equivalent fractions, some according to colour. This is a good activity which can be used to introduce the part–whole concept of fractions so that you can assess their understanding of what a fraction is. It also provides the opportunity to make simple addition and subtraction calculations as described above.

Quotient model for fractions

The quotient model is a division model; for example, if I have one cake and I share it between two, we could say 1 divided by 2. We would each have half. When looking at the quotient model, writing the numerator first to show how many we have, then the vinculum to show we are dividing and then the denominator to show how many we are dividing into is often clearer. Using real items is helpful, for example, cakes or slices of bread. Children should draw models as well.

If we have two cakes and share them among three people, the division calculation would be 2 divided by 3 which gives each person one third of each cake so two thirds in total. We can show this using simple diagrams, such as the following.

Diagram 2.15

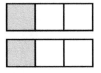

The following approach is one children may take.

This approach is trickier because the children end up with each person having half of one cake and a third of a half of the other. This leaves a tricky calculation to find the total amount of cake each person will have. Encouraging children to find the fraction of each whole, as in the first model, would be best. However, we could model both and ask the children which they think is the clearest.

Fractions as numbers

Fractions are cardinal and ordinal numbers. Cardinal indicates the amount, so Sophie might have one fourth of a cake. Ordinal numbers show the order. Fractions can and should be positioned on a number line. There is only one position on a number line for whole numbers. For example, 2 always comes after 1 and before 3; no other whole numbers are positioned in the same place. On the other hand, an infinite number of fractions can be placed in the same position when we consider equivalence; for example, one half is at the same position as two fourths, three sixths, four eighths and so on. These fractions will all be positioned exactly between zero and 1.

Diagram 2.16

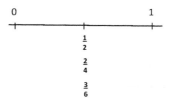

We should be counting in fractions. In the notes and guidance section of the Year 2 fractions curriculum, it suggests that children count in halves and quarters to reinforce the concept of fractions as numbers that can add up to more than one. It also familiarises children with mixed numbers and improper fractions. For example, if counting one, one and a half, two, two and a half, three, three and a half, we can ask children how many halves are equivalent to three and a half. This would only work, however, if we are using a good visual representation or if they are using manipulatives, such as interlocking cubes as they count, they should be able to see that seven halves are equivalent to three wholes and one half.

Diagram 2.17

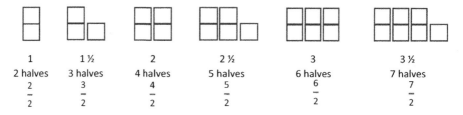

Fractions as operators

To find two thirds of a number or quantity, we find one third by dividing the amount by three and then find two thirds by multiplying the size of one third by two. Sadly, this seems to be the focus of much of the fractions teaching in Key Stage 1, possibly due to the Standard Assessment Test papers (https://www.gov.uk/government/organisations/standards-and-testing-agency) which asks children to, for example, circle a particular fraction of dots or find a fraction of a number. This is an important area within this topic but is by no means the most important one.

Fractions of quantities

When we find fractions of quantities, it is important that we give children the opportunity to explore a range of items. Excellent connections to measurement can be made through these explorations. On several occasions, with different year groups, we have explored fractions of strips of paper of different lengths, lengths of string, bottles of water, different amounts of money, different numbers of counters and so on. This has involved measuring lengths using rulers, different volumes using measuring jugs, different masses using balance scales. In Years 2 and 3, they folded strips of paper that were 15 cm long and measured half. They labelled half with $7\frac{1}{2}$ cm in Year 2 and 7.5 cm in Year 3, making that connection to tenths from place value. After exploring half, they then went on to explore fourths of the same items to make the link that a fourth is half of one half.

Fractions of shape

For decades, we have been giving examples of fractions of shape where the shapes all look the same. This has led to misconceptions that fractions are all about appearance. In fact, fractions of shape are about the amount of space, or area, they take up. Fractions are introduced in the national curriculum in Year 1 and area in Year 4. Children in Year 1 need to be aware that an area is a space, so the carpet area is the amount of space in the classroom that they sit on and the book corner is the area in the classroom where the books are kept. A simple way to demonstrate area is to give each child a six-by-six-square grid and ask them to shade nine squares in a different pattern from their partner. Look at all the examples they come up with. They will have shaded one fourth of the square in many different ways so proving that the same fraction can be different in appearance.

We should give children not only standard examples of fractions of shape but also less standard examples. These conceptual variations will deepen understanding.

Diagram 2.18

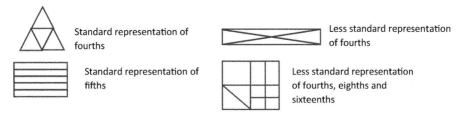

A few years ago, I gave a class of Year 5 children copies of this less standard representation of fourths.

I wanted them to prove that they were fourths. All of them said that it was impossible because the triangles were different shapes and therefore couldn't be the same fraction. I encouraged them to have a go because they were really all fourths. Only two children managed to do it. They cut and folded the representation and eventually discovered that each fourth could be cut into two eighths which all had the same area (and looked the same).

I repeated this in Year 3, and all the children were happy to try. Many were able to prove that there were fourths, and they came up with several different ways to do this.

That told me that the misconception about fractions being identical shapes does not arise until the children are working their way through Key Stage 2.

The following photograph shows a Year 4 child's work when identifying fractions of shape that do not look the same.

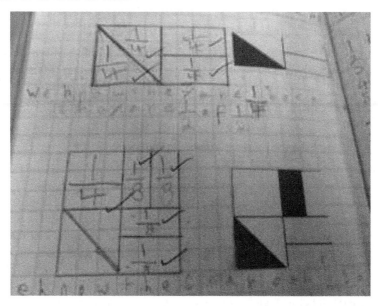

Equivalence

As mentioned previously, equivalence is a natural extension of a child's exploration of simple fractions. By using visual resources, they should be able to tell you how many of a fraction is equivalent to one whole and how many fourths are equivalent to one half. However, there comes a time in Key Stage 2 when they need to use multiplication and division to find equivalent fractions. Visuals such as the following help.

Diagram 2.19

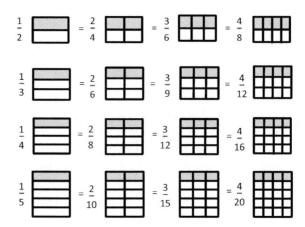

When showing each set of equivalences, it is important to ask the children what is the same and what is different. Basically, they are the same value but have a different appearance. Ask them if they can see a pattern and if they can predict what the next equivalent fraction will be and why. The aim is to help the children understand that to make equivalent fractions, they need to multiply or divide the numerator and the denominator by the same integer. However, it is important that they work out this generalisation for themselves. We should not simply tell them. Telling them does not lead to a depth of understanding.

In upper Key Stage 2, children will be adding fractions in which they need to find common denominators, so their understanding of how to find equivalent fractions before then is important. These are looked at in more depth when calculating with fractions is considered.

Improper fractions and mixed numbers

If the children have been counting in fractions from, for example, zero to 10, in the way previously described, they will be familiar with mixed numbers and improper fractions. When adding fractions with sums greater than one, as is expected in Year 4, children will need to change the improper fractions to mixed numbers. Currently, this is a requirement for Year 5, but teaching it when it is appropriate makes sense.

We can see that we have seven thirds.

$\frac{1}{3}$	$\frac{1}{3}$	$\frac{1}{3}$	$\frac{1}{3}$	$\frac{1}{3}$	$\frac{1}{3}$	$\frac{1}{3}$

Three thirds make one whole; another three thirds make one whole, which is a total of two wholes; and there is one third left. So, seven thirds is equivalent to two and one third.

$\frac{1}{3}$	$\frac{1}{3}$	$\frac{1}{3}$	$\frac{1}{3}$	$\frac{1}{3}$	$\frac{1}{3}$	$\frac{1}{3}$

We could link this with integers: seven equals three add three add one, so seven thirds is three thirds add three thirds add one third.

At some point, the children need to develop a generalisation for changing an improper fraction to a mixed number and vice versa. After lots of investigation and practical work, they should be able to notice that to change an improper fraction to a mixed number we can divide the numerator by the denominator. The whole-number part of the quotient is the number of wholes, and the remainder is the numerator. In the following example, 2 is divided into 5 to give 2 remainder 1, which is two and a half.

$$\frac{5}{2} = 2\frac{1}{2}$$

To convert from a mixed number to an improper fraction, the whole number is multiplied by the denominator, and the numerator is added, for example, $3\frac{2}{5}$.

Three is multiplied by 5 to give 15 and the numerator of 2 is added to give an improper fraction of $\frac{17}{5}$.

Calculating with fractions

The national curriculum requires that children add and subtract fractions with the same denominator within one whole in Years 3 and 4. The notes and guidance suggest that, in Year 4, they should be adding and subtracting beyond 1. In actual fact, if being taught effectively, children in Key Stage 1 have been adding and subtracting fractions with the same denominator in their explorations of the part–whole model for two years. If they have a real understanding of fractions as equal parts of one whole, they should be able to understand that if one whole is divided into six equal parts, each part is one sixth, and if adding one sixth and two sixths, the sum will be three sixths.

Surely, Year 3 is the time for the children to explore adding and subtracting fractions with denominators that are multiples of the same number? This is an expectation for Year 5; I would suggest that by then, children should be adding and subtracting more unrelated fractions by finding common denominators. Often, too much is left until Year 6, when the end-of-key-stage-test pressure is on, and children still have new learning to cover. If this happens, rules tend to be taught and understanding is not achieved.

Using visual resources, similar to the one that follows, children are able to add and subtract with denominators that are multiples of the same number without too much difficulty. In Year 3, the children begin by exploring equivalence and can clearly see that one half is equivalent to two fourths. They run their fingers along the half part, drop down to the fourth line, add one and notice that adding those two fractions together will give them three fourths. They explore the fact that they can make one half equivalent to two fourths and make the addition two fourths add one fourth, which gives a sum of three fourths. They could then run their fingers along to one fourth, drop down and add one eighth to give three eighths. They make the link that one fourth is equivalent to two eighths, and so this calculation would be two eighths add one eighth, which gives a sum of three eighths. This helps them to understand that to add fractions, the denominators must be the same.

Diagram 2.20

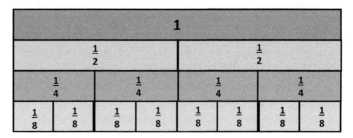

I would repeat this with thirds, sixths and twelfths, and children would subtract in a similar way. So, if the calculation was one half subtract one fourth. They would run their finger along one half again and, this time, drop down and go back one fourth. They would make the link that one half is equivalent to two fourths, so the calculation would be two fourths subtract one fourth, giving a difference of one fourth.

In Year 4, they would continue adding and subtracting these fractions, recapping within one whole and then move on to beyond one whole, for example, one half add three fourths. They convert the half to quarters to make the calculation two fourths add three fourths, which is equivalent to five fourths. They would then convert the improper fraction to the mixed number of one and one fourth. For subtraction, they would consider, for example, one and three eighths subtract three fourths. This time, everything needs to be converted to eighths to make the calculation eleven eighths subtract six eighths, which gives a difference of five eighths:

$$1\frac{3}{8} - \frac{3}{4} = \frac{11}{8} - \frac{6}{8} = \frac{5}{8}$$

The following is an example of work carried out in a Year 4 classroom after recapping addition and subtraction with the same denominator. This also involved converting improper fractions to mixed numbers.

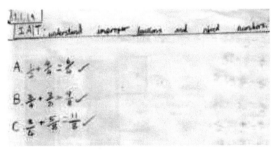

If children are following a progression like this, they will be ready to explore adding and subtracting fractions that do not have denominators that are multiples of the same number.

Following are two examples of work carried out in a Year 3 classroom.

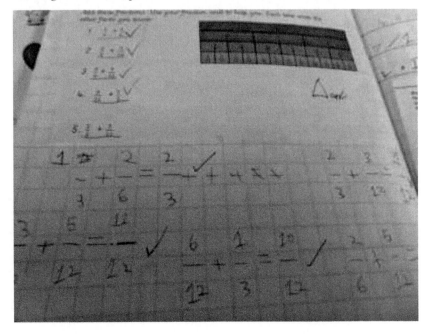

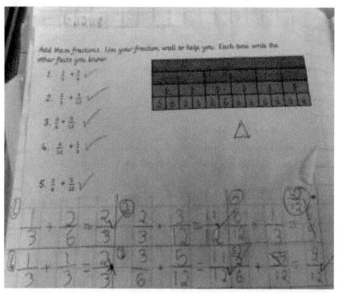

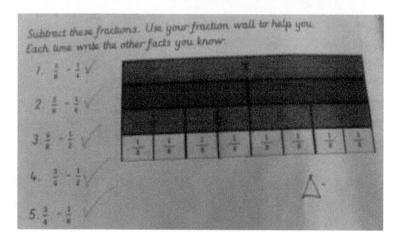

Following a model similar to that for finding equivalent fractions, as previously described, children will be able to make a generalisation for finding common denominators. They should begin exploring this with unit fractions (fractions with numerators of one). If children add one half and one third, they need to find a common denominator. From the model that follows, we can see that the common denominator is six; now they can add three sixths and two sixths to make five sixths. With plenty of practice, they should see that to find the common denominator they multiply the two denominators together. Again, that they work out the generalisation for themselves is very important. When confident, they could start finding the lowest common denominator. Of course, they need to be fluent with their multiplication facts to do this efficiently! When working on multiples and factors, linking these to common denominators and rehearsing addition and subtraction of fractions are helpful.

Diagram 2.21

$$\frac{1}{2} \quad = \quad \frac{2}{4} \quad = \quad \frac{3}{6}$$

$$\frac{1}{3} \quad = \quad \frac{2}{6}$$

After they have mastered addition and subtraction of unit fractions, they will move onto non-unit fractions (fractions with numerators that are not 1). For example, if children add one half and two thirds, their first job is to find the common denominator. They need to remember that they found the common denominator for adding one half and one third. Now they are adding two thirds so, because they multiplied the denominator by two to make sixths, they must multiply the numerator by 2 to give four sixths. This is the same as the generalisation that the children developed for finding equivalent fractions. The main difference here is finding the common denominator first.

By the time children enter Year 6, they should have mastered addition and subtraction of fractions, so they should only need to recap and rehearse this area of mathematics.

In Year 5, children begin multiplying fractions by whole numbers. This is quite straightforward if children remember that multiplication is also repeated addition. I have taught this in Year 5, and children can make and understand the generalisation very quickly without being told what it is.

We used Cuisenaire rods, but counters or anything similar can be used. The children set three rods in front of them. I asked, 'If each rod is worth 25, what is the product?' They answered that and then showed me the multiplication and repeated addition statements that could be made. We did this a few times for whole numbers and then moved onto fractions in the same way. If each rod is one half, the product is three halves; if each rod is three fourths, the product will be three fourths add three fourths and another three fourths to give a product of twelve fourths:

$$\frac{3}{4} \times 4 = \frac{3}{4} + \frac{3}{4} + \frac{3}{4} + \frac{3}{4} = \frac{12}{4}$$

They also proved the products by folding strips of paper to make the fraction and show it three times. They worked on the examples that follow, some of which show some procedural variation: the same multiplier for several and repeating the fraction when the multiplier changed.

1. $\dfrac{1}{3} \times 4$ 5. $\dfrac{1}{3} \times 5$ 9. $\dfrac{1}{6} \times 6$
     $\times 4$ $\times 5$ $\times 6$

2. $\dfrac{2}{3} \times 4$ 6. $\dfrac{2}{3} \times 5$ 10. $\dfrac{5}{6} \times 6$
     $\times 4$ $\times 5$ $\times 6$

3. $\dfrac{1}{5} \times 4$ 7. $\dfrac{1}{5} \times 5$ 11. $\dfrac{3}{8} \times 6$
     $\times 4$ $\times 5$ $\times 6$

4. $\dfrac{2}{5} \times 4$ 8. $\dfrac{2}{5} \times 5$ 12. $\dfrac{5}{8} \times 6$
     $\times 4$ $\times 5$ $\times 6$

The whole class did this, and all worked confidently. This was the first time they had encountered this concept; therefore, I wanted to ensure they could all complete the task. We were focusing on multiplying, so I did not necessarily want them to convert the product to mixed numbers. However, some children chose to do this, which was fine. Those who worked through the task quickly went on to make up their own examples, choosing their own fractions and multipliers.

Towards the end of the lesson, we took a look at the improper fraction products; I wanted the children to tell me what they noticed. They noticed that they could multiply the numerator by the multiplier to give the product, which is a useful generalisation. That children discover this for themselves is really important.

1. $\dfrac{1}{3} \times 4 = \dfrac{4}{3}$

2. $\dfrac{2}{3} \times 4 = \dfrac{8}{3}$

3. $\dfrac{1}{5} \times 4 = \dfrac{4}{5}$

4. $\dfrac{2}{5} \times 4 = \dfrac{8}{5}$

I have had conversations with a few teachers about turning the multiplier into a fraction, giving it a denominator of one, which is something they said they did. They then told the children that all they needed to do was multiply the numerators and the denominators to get the product. This is totally unnecessary and changes the national curriculum requirement to multiplying fractions by fractions instead of whole numbers. Multiplying fractions by fractions is the requirement for Year 6.

In Year 6, children are expected to multiply fractions by fractions. This is not a repeated addition model as when multiplying by whole numbers; it is more of a scaling model. So, children mastering the concepts of scaling up and down is important. Scaling is looked at in the section on multiplicative reasoning.

One misconception the children develop is that multiplication always gives a product that is higher than the multiplicand and multiplier. It is therefore important that we show this is not always the case. Showing them examples like this is helpful:

$2 \times 3 = 6$

$2 \times 2 = 4$

$2 \times 1 = 2$

Ask the children what they notice and then ask what they think the product will be if we multiply 2 by one half and then one quarter. In this way they will understand that multiplying can give a product that can be smaller.

If we take one fourth and multiply it by one half, we are making one fourth half the size. We could also look at this the other way around and make one half, one fourth of the size. Multiplication of fractions is commutative, just like whole numbers.

There are at least two good models for the children to use when exploring this. One of them is folding strips of paper. For example, they take a strip of paper and fold it into four equal parts. They then fold the result in half again and shade the result. They open their strip and can see that half of one fourth is one eighth.

Diagram 2.22

$$\frac{1}{4} \times \frac{1}{2} = \frac{1}{8}$$

They could also draw a grid and divide that into four equal parts in one direction and then in half in the other direction.

Diagram 2.23

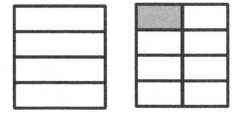

We can see from this model that one half of one fourth is one eighth and that one fourth of one half is one eighth.

This 'grid' model is helpful when the fractions are more complex and folding strips of paper is difficult. Children begin multiplying unit fractions and then move on to non-unit fractions.

Diagram 2.24

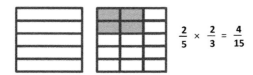

$$\frac{2}{5} \times \frac{2}{3} = \frac{4}{15}$$

After lots of exploration with the expectation that children record the calculations, ask the children what they notice. They should be able to tell you that the product can be made by multiplying the numerators together and the denominators together.

As with multiplying by whole numbers, that children are given the opportunity to explore and to make and understand the generalisation for themselves is so important. Too many teachers just teach the rule, which does not help deepen a child's understanding. From speaking to Year 6 teachers, I know that this often happens because of the pressure of the Year 6 standard assessment test. If we can develop a sensible progression through fractions from Year R, such as the one described earlier, children will have a far better understanding of fractions by the time they arrive in Year 6, and their teachers will have time to let them explore how multiplying fractions by fractions works.

In Year 6, children are also required to divide fractions by whole numbers. We do not need to teach them how to divide fractions by fractions. For some reason, a few Year 6 teachers do this. They also teach them how to do this by using the KFC method: keep, flip, calculate (by multiplying) – a rule which makes absolutely no sense! I am still waiting to meet someone who can explain why this rule was introduced and to give me the proof that it develops a depth of understanding of this concept. Most of us were taught this method when we were at school. The national curriculum requires us to teach dividing fractions by whole numbers. So teaching this 'trick' in Year 6 is totally unnecessary.

As always, children need to understand how dividing fractions by whole numbers works, and the only way to do that is to explore this concept practically. It could be argued that this is a sharing model. Begin with unit fractions and build this concept slowly. If asking children to, for example, divide one half by two, give children strips of paper and ask them to show half, share that into two equal parts and shade one. They should be able to see that one half divided by two is equivalent to one fourth.

Diagram 2.25

They could also draw their own models.

$$\frac{1}{2} \div 2 = \frac{1}{4}$$

$$\frac{1}{3} \div 4 = \frac{1}{12}$$

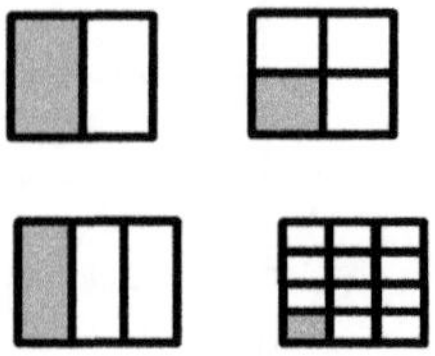

The aim would be for the children to notice that the denominator is multiplied by the divisor.

When children understand this, they move on to non-unit fractions and investigate whether the generalisation is the same. They will see that it is.

$$\frac{2}{5} \div 2 = \frac{2}{10}$$

Decimals

A decimal is a fraction whose denominator is a power of 10. Its numerator is the numeral or numerals positioned to the right of the decimal point. As mentioned in the Place Value section, teaching decimals within the context of place value makes sense. We should expect children to compare, order and round decimal numbers, as well as whole numbers, throughout Key Stage 2.

Adding and subtracting numbers with decimals when teaching addition and subtraction also makes sense. I teach addition and subtraction for numbers with one decimal place in Year 3 and two decimal places in Year 4. We begin with whole numbers and then practise within the context of length. Children need to understand that decimals work in the same way that whole numbers do when carrying out the four operations. This is considered further in the Additive Reasoning and Multiplicative Reasoning sections of this book.

In Year 6, the national curriculum requires children to identify the value of each digit in numbers given to three decimal places and multiply and divide numbers by 10, 100 and 1000, giving answers up to three decimal places. This concept will have been covered in Year 5 during children's place-value work. They will have begun multiplying and dividing numbers by ten in place value work from Year 1 or 2, linking to tenths in Year 3, multiplying and dividing by 100 in Year 4 and linking to hundredths. Therefore, this should not be a new concept to the children.

Anyone following the advice in this book will have explored multiplying numbers with up to two decimal places by whole numbers in Year 5. The national curriculum requirement of this is for Year 6. However, teaching it during multiplication and division so that, again, children can make the link that multiplying numbers with decimal places is no different to multiplying whole numbers makes sense. This is considered further during the section on multiplicative reasoning.

In Year 6, the new learning is to use written division methods in cases in which the answer has up to two decimal places. By now, children should be familiar with adding, subtracting and multiplying decimals, so dividing is a natural next step. Again, this is looked at more closely in the Multiplicative Reasoning section.

Percentages

A percentage is another type of fraction. It describes a number out of 100. We have considered introducing the children to percentages in Year 4 when looking at hundredths because they will be familiar with them from their lives outside of school. In Year 5, they begin to calculate with them. In the national curriculum for Year 6, it specifically states that children need to calculate percentages in the ratio and proportion section of the national curriculum. In Year 5, the national curriculum for fractions appears to focus on recognising and understanding what a percentage is and writing percentages as fractions with a denominator of 100 and as a decimal. In Year 6, the focus is on recalling and using equivalences among fractions, decimals and percentages, which is clearly not much of a progression from Year 5!

When working out percentages of amounts, it is helpful to find 10% and then double, halve, multiply and divide by 10, add and subtract to make other percentages. I find that children are not very flexible in their methods, so if we teach them a rule such as divide the number by 100 and multiply by the percentage, this is what most of them will always do. This is what a great many of us were taught to do when we were at school! What we want is to encourage flexible, and therefore deeper, thinking.

I like to give children an amount of money that is equivalent to 100%, say, for example, that £240. They then find different percentages in a given time by dividing by ten and then doubling, halving, adding and subtracting. If they start with 10% is equivalent to £24, 5% is half, so giving £12; 15% is equivalent to 10% and 5%, so will be £36; 20% is double 10%, and so is £48; and so on. This is great practice for mental calculation strategies, which are looked at more closely later in this book.

We also need to ask children percentage-related problems, such as the coat problem mentioned in an earlier part of this section.

This was a percentage problem from the 2018 Standard Assessment Test paper.

Jack has £400.

He spends 35% of his money on a new bike.

> How much does Jack spend on his new bike?

Children can find 10% and multiply by 3 for 30%. They can halve 10% for 5% and then add that to £120 to calculate Jack's spend on his bike as £140.

Ideally, this kind of work on percentages should happen in Year 5 and then be recapped in Year 6.

In the 2018 Standard Assessment Test for arithmetic there were three percentage questions. The first was 20% of 1200. Finding 10% and doubling is the most obvious way to answer this. The second was 99% of 200. Playing around with 10% is not the most obvious way. Because 99% is so close to 100%, children could find 1% and subtract that. However, they should have known that 99% of 100 is 99, so 99% of 200 would simply be double 99. The third question was 28% of 650. Finding 10% is useful here: 10% of 650 is 65, so 20% is 130, 1% is 6.5 and multiply that by 8 to give 52. Therefore, 28% would be 182.

An interesting fact that always works for percentages is that we can 'flip' them and get the same answer. So, if we needed to work out 8% of 75, we could work out 75% of 8, and we would get the answer to 8% of 75. Finding 75% of 8 is easier because it is three quarters of 8 which is 6. Both answers are 6. Why? Because 8% is $\frac{8}{100}$, if we multiply that by 75, we will get $\frac{600}{100}$, which is equivalent to 6. 75% is $\frac{75}{100}$, if we multiply that by 8, we get the same result due to the law of commutativity. This law enables us to look at finding a percentage of an amount in two ways and choose the one which is the easiest!

Linking fractions, decimals and percentages

As mentioned previously, linking fractions, decimals and percentages is a focus in Years 5 and 6. Many children struggle with this area, but if we taught these as they arise, then, I am fairly sure, fewer would have problems. Looking at fraction and decimal equivalences should begin in Year 3, with tenths in place value, continue in Year 4, with hundredths, and the link to percentages then into Year 5, with thousandths. In Years 5 and 6, children need to explore the links between other fractions, for example, half, fourths, fifths and eighths. They could do this by using what they already know; for example, they know that five tenths are equivalent to one half, so one half must be 0.5 and 50%. One half is equivalent to two fourths, so one fourth must be 0.25 and 25%. One fourth is equivalent to two eighths, so one eighth must be 0.125 and $12\frac{1}{2}$%. Two tenths are equivalent to one fifth, so must be 0.2 and 20%. In this way, all the fourth, fifths and eighths can be converted to decimals and percentages.

Ratio and proportion

A ratio is the relationship between two or more groups, values or amounts that expresses how much bigger one is than the other or others. It can be represented in different ways. We often use a colon to separate values. For example, one for every two can be shown as 1:2. A ratio can be represented as a fraction that separates one value from the total. It can be represented as a decimal, after dividing one value by the total and as a percentage. It also represents the quantitative relationship between two amounts that shows how many times greater one value is than the other. This final representation fits in with scaling up and scaling down. This is looked at more closely in the multiplicative reasoning section of this book.

In the national curriculum for Year 6, ratio and proportion have their own section, which makes them look like different concepts, despite the fact that percentages and fractions are mentioned in those requirements. In the days of the National Numeracy

Strategy (NNS), fractions, decimals, percentages, ratio and proportion were all linked. That they are separated is a shame because they are all ways of representing relationships. I believe ratios actually begin not in Year 6 but in Year R, with doubling and halving, and continues into Key Stage 1, with scaling, solving problems such as 'Bertie has two apples, Freddie has twice as many. How many apples do they have altogether?' Proportion is basically a fraction, a part of something compared to the whole.

One of the best resources for helping children make sense of ratios is simply counters. When practically using counters, children should also be encouraged to draw a diagram, for example, circles. If children get into the habit of making and drawing, they will be able to draw representations in test circumstances. The following question is from the 2017 Standard Assessment Test.

Amina planted some seeds.

For every 3 seeds Amina planted, only 2 seeds grew.

Altogether, 12 seeds grew.

How many seeds did Amina **plant**?

Many children were not successful with this question. If they had been used to using manipulatives and visual representations, they might have drawn something similar to the following diagram and achieved the correct answer.

Diagram 2.26

The two counters represent the 12 seeds that grow. Therefore, each counter must be worth 6 seeds: 6 multiplied by 5 is 30. So, she planted 30 seeds. Easy!

Another way of looking at this could be to turn the ratio into the fractions $\frac{2}{5}$ and $\frac{3}{5}$. If $\frac{2}{5}$ is 12, then $\frac{1}{5}$ must be 6, making the whole 30.

Solving fraction-related problems

Bar modelling is an ideal visual representation that enables children to solve quite complex fraction problems. The following are a few examples.

I have asked several classes of Year 1 to solve such problems as 'Sophie had some grapes. She ate half of them and had two left. How many did she start off with?' The children showed the problem using strips of paper. They folded their strip in half and wrote 2 on the part she had left. They could see from this that Sophie must have eaten two grapes and therefore started with four.

2	2

In addition to solving the problem, they made the link to doubling. After the children practised this with strips of paper, I gave them plain paper and asked them to sketch their own bars without using rulers. Insisting on using rulers to draw lines distracts children from problem solving. This process worked really well because the children have physically made the bar model and therefore have a model to copy. We kept the problem the same and just varied the amounts of grapes she has left. I then asked them to draw the whole bar underneath the parts and to fill that with the number of grapes Sophie started off with.

They then made up their own numbers of grapes, keeping the numbers simple if they wanted to or using more complicated numbers if they wanted to challenge themselves. One boy decided to have 99 as the number of grapes that Sophie had left. We were wondering where he was going to go with this! He told us that 99 is close to 100, so he could double 100 and subtract 2. Not bad for a child in the autumn term of Year 1! Letting children make up their own calculations can show us a lot about what they are able to do.

In Year 2, we should ask the children to solve problems, such as 'Bertie had some marbles. He gave one half of them to Tommy and one fourth to Amy. He was left with 5. How many marbles did he start off with?' I have given a similar problem to children in Year 2, and initially. they folded strips of paper into half and labelled one half T for Tommy. They folded the strip in half again, for fourths, and labelled one with A for Amy. In the remaining part, they wrote 5. They could now see that Amy must have 5, Tommy must have 10 and Bertie must have started with 20. Again, this links well with doubling.

5	5	10
20		

After practising with paper strips, they draw the model as in Year 1. We began by giving them numbers, increasing in size and then, they made up their own numbers.

The following is a Level 5 Key Stage 2 Standard Assessment Test question from 2016, which a lot of Year 6 children answered incorrectly.

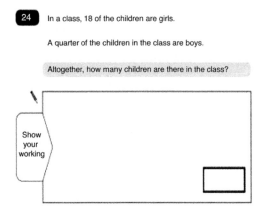

I now give this to Year 3 children because I believe that with the right approach and visualisations, they can solve questions like this. We begin with double-sided counters.

Diagram 2.27

I ask questions such as the following:

- The four counters represent 24. What fraction does each part represent? What is the value of each part? What is the value of three fourths?
- If one fourth is three, what are three fourths? What is the whole?

I then ask them to show one fourth using the counters.

We then solve some similar problems using the counters and then drawing bar models. For example,

In Year 3, $\frac{1}{4}$ of the children are boys. There are 30 girls. How many children are in Year 3? Using the model, the children could clearly see that, if three parts represented 30, then one part must be ten. So, there must be 10 boys and 40 children in Year 3.

B	G	G	G
Year 3			

10	10	10	10
40			

We then add variation to the problem:

What if there were 24 girls? What if there were 33 girls? What if there were 36 girls? What if there were 48 girls?

We repeat the same problem but vary the fraction: In a Year 3 class, $\frac{3}{4}$ of the children are boys; In a Year 3 class, $\frac{2}{5}$ of the children are boys.

They then solve the SAT (standard assessment test) question.

The children could access this problem with the counters and the bar model; the only issue, for some, was the division. So, the next time I worked on this with a Year 3 class, I gave them calculators to use to carry out the arithmetic. When we teach, we need to ensure we are clear on the purpose of the lesson. If it is problem solving, we want them to focus on that and not let the arithmetic get in the way so give them calculators. If it is calculating, we should not give them calculators, except maybe for checking using the inverse. This is discussed further in the next section.

In Year 4, we should be asking problems such as 'Sam spent $\frac{2}{5}$ of his money on a book. The book cost £10. How much money did he start with?'

When I first broached this problem a few years ago with a class of Year 5, this type of problem solving was new for them. In fact, when I shared it with them, some of them looked horrified: problem + fractions + money = nightmare! So, we began with counters. They used 5 and turned 2 over to represent the amount spent on the book. The 2 represented £10, so each counter must represent £5 and Sam started with £25. As we practised, all the children could see it made absolute sense and were happy to pursue the problem solving.

Most went on to draw bar models similar to the one below.

£5	£5	£5	£5	£5
£25				

Again, we varied the problem by varying the cost of the book and then the fraction Sam spent. I have repeated this several times, successfully with Year 4. As before, if any children wanted to use a calculator to calculate more complex amounts, they were available for them to use.

In Year 5, appropriate problems could include 'Grace baked some biscuits. She put two thirds of them into a container. She gave one fourth of what was left to her friend. She had 30 left. How many biscuits did she bake?'

We encouraged the children to draw a drop-down bar to work out one fourth of one third by modelling this first.

Diagram 2.28

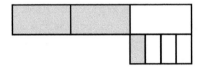

From this model, the children can see that each of the fourths must be 10; therefore, one third is equivalent to 40. So, she must have baked 120 biscuits. We varied the number of biscuits and then the fraction that she gave to her friend.

From my experience, some children do not need to use the drop-down bar. They can solve the problem by directly making the one third into fourths. From this, they can see that one of the three thirds must be 40.

Showing them the drop-down is good practice for future problems that need it.

For example, I have given a problem similar to the following to Year 6. We began with a simpler problem to demonstrate the drop-down part of the bar model. Then the children worked on the problem:

> The shop sold one fifth of its boxes of cat food in the first week of March. It sold two thirds of what was left in the second week of March. There were 12 boxes left. How many boxes did the shop have before selling any?

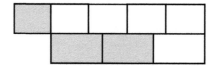

From this model, the children can see that the drop-down bar has a value of 36 (three lots of 12 boxes). This means that four of the fifths also has a value of 36. One fifth is therefore 9. So, the shop began with 45 boxes of cat food.

When working on the problem I gave to Year 6, I noticed one girl working very systematically, and I asked her if she would be prepared to demonstrate how she found the solution. She agreed and beautifully explained, drawing the bar model as she did. At the end of the lesson, the teacher told me that the girl was one of her lower-attaining pupils! I believe her explanation proved that she wasn't.

The bar model for fractions opens up complex word problems and makes them so much more accessible to everyone.

Fractions and percentages with pie charts

The national curriculum requires children in Year 6 to interpret and construct pie charts and line graphs and use these to solve problems. We consider line graphs in the section on additive reasoning.

A pie chart is a chart that uses what look like pie slice sections to show the relative size of particular data. These need an understanding of angles, fractions and percentages in order for them to be interpreted. It therefore makes perfect sense to link pie charts to fractions and percentages and also to geometric reasoning.

In the Year 6 Standard Assessment Tests for reasoning, every year or so is a question that involves solving problems with pie charts. In 2018, in the second reasoning paper, the following appeared.

This chart shows the number of different types of big cats in a zoo.

There are **20** big cats in the zoo altogether.

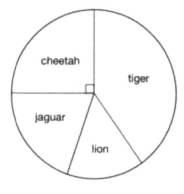

Here are some statements about the chart.

The children were asked to tick the statements that are true.

There are more cheetahs than jaguars.	☐
The total number of lions and tigers is 10.	☐
One quarter of the big cats are cheetahs.	☐
There are more than 5 jaguars.	☐

The children should be able to tell you that one fourth or one quarter of the cats are cheetahs and this represents 25% of the whole. The whole is 20, so one fourth or 25% is 5, which means there must be five cheetahs. The children should be able to deduce that there are more cheetahs than jaguars from looking at the sizes of the two sections, so there cannot be more than five jaguars. A good estimate of the number of jaguars would be four. The total of lions and tigers is more than half, so therefore, there are more than 10.

Children should be able to visualise that approximately one third of the lion section could be added to the jaguar section to make one fourth. If there are four jaguars, then the lion part would be 1. In total, there would be three lions. If we add the parts worked out so far, we would have 12 cats. That means there would be eight tigers. We could highlight that four twentieths, or one fifth, are jaguars, which is 20%; eight twentieths, or two fifths, are tigers, which is 40%; and three twentieths are lions, which must be 15%. Adding these parts together along with the 25% of cats which are cheetahs gives the whole, which is 100%.

Examples such as the preceding one provide a great opportunity to link this statistical work to fractions and percentages. I would recommend using SATs-style questions as a way into teaching this concept.

The 2013 SATs paper 2 gave the following problem.

Megan asked children from two different schools,

'How do you travel to school?'

Here are her results.

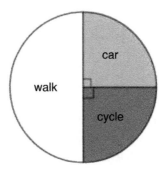

Foxwood school
80 children

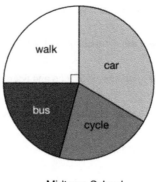

Midtown School
240 children

Megan says,

**'The number of children walking to Foxwood School is
more than the number walking to Midtown School.'**

Is she correct?
Circle **Yes** or **No**.   Yes / No

Explain how you know,

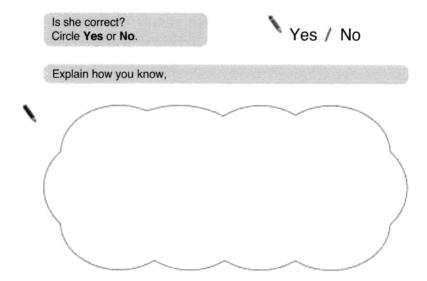

For this part of the problem, children should be able to identify that there are one half,
or 50%, walking to Foxwood School and one fourth, or 25%, walking to Midtown
School. One half of 80 is 40, and one fourth of 240 is 60, so despite the appearance
on the parts in both pie charts, more children walk to Midtown School; Megan is
incorrect. Children must be aware of the value of the whole pie chart to answer this
correctly.

At Midtown school, one third of children travel by car.

The number of children who cycle is the same as the number who go on the bus.

How many children **cycle** to Midtown School?

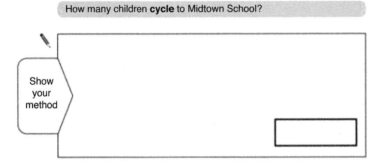

If 60 children walk to Midtown School and one third, or 80 children, travel by car, the remaining 100 children must either cycle or travel to school by bus. An equal number of children are cycling and taking the bus, so each part must have a value of 50. Therefore, 50 children cycle to school.

This is another SATs problem from 2012, paper 1.

This pie chart shows the ingredients to make a food mixture for wild birds.

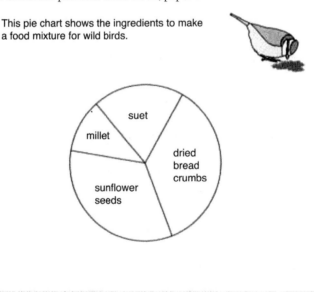

Estimate the **percentage** of mixture that is suet.

%

To answer this problem, children need to understand that 100% represents all the different foods in the mixture for the birds. You would expect children to look at the suet section of the pie and visualise that it is a slightly less than one fourth, or 25%. A sensible estimate would be 20%. The mark scheme allows for a range of answers between 15% and 25%.

Mina uses 100 grams of millet in the mixture.

Estimate how many grams of sunflower seeds she should use.

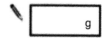

For the second part of the problem, you would expect children to be able to visualise that the size of the sunflower section is approximately three times the size of the millet section. So, if there are 100 g of millet, there must be about 300 g of sunflower seeds. The mark scheme accepts an answer within the range of 200 g to 400 g.

Children also need to construct their own pie charts. At first, they could simply draw a circle and then show half, quarter and eighth. They could make up their own problem that involves 50%, 25% and 12.5%. They could move onto using a circular protractor, draw round it and put marks at, for example, 45°, 90°, 135°, 180°, 225°, 270°, 315° and 360°. They could make eight parts, each part one eighth or 12.5%. They could then combine these parts to make different fractions and percentages, for example, two eighths to give 25% or three eighths to give 37.5%. They can then make up and solve problems. From my search of the SATs papers from 2000 to 2018, I have not found any questions that ask the children to construct a pie chart but as it is a requirement one may come up sometime.

Suggested progression for teaching fractions

The following table sums up a suggested progression in fractions that we are working on in some schools. We hope you will find it helpful.

Year R	**Part whole:** simple, practical exploration of parts and wholes within contexts such as picnics **Equivalence:** simple equivalence to one whole, using manipulatives and visualisations and others to be discussed during practical problem-solving activities **Addition and subtraction:** making one whole with halves, quarters and other fractions used in sharing activities
Year 1	**Part whole:** simple, practical exploration of unequal parts and wholes, leading to equal parts and wholes **Equivalence:** simple equivalence to one whole and half, using manipulatives and visualisations **Addition and subtraction:** making one whole for different fractions with the same denominator, include commutativity and inverse
Year 2	**Part whole:** practically rehearse exploration of unequal parts and wholes, leading to equal parts and wholes **Equivalence:** simple equivalence to one whole, half, fourths, etc. using manipulatives and visualisations **Addition and subtraction:** adding and subtracting fractions less than one with the same denominator, including commutativity and inverse

Year 3	**Part whole:** rehearse unequal parts and wholes and equal parts and wholes **Equivalence:** simple equivalence using manipulatives and visualisations, beginning to explore the generalisation **Addition and subtraction:** adding and subtracting fractions within one with denominators that are multiples of the same number
Year 4	**Part whole:** rehearse unequal parts and wholes and equal parts and wholes **Equivalence:** simple equivalence using manipulatives and visualisations, develop and consolidate the generalisation **Mixed numbers and improper fractions:** develop an understanding of these and how to convert from one to the other **Addition and subtraction:** as Year 3 but including mixed and improper fractions greater than one
Year 5	**Part whole:** consolidate unequal parts and wholes and equal parts and wholes **Equivalence:** consolidate the generalisation **Mixed numbers and improper fractions:** develop the generalisation for converting from one to the other **Addition and subtraction:** adding and subtracting any fractions by finding common denominators **Multiplication and division:** multiplying fractions by whole numbers
Year 6	**Part whole:** consolidate unequal parts and wholes and equal parts and wholes **Equivalence:** consolidate the generalisation **Mixed numbers and improper fractions:** consolidate the generalisation for converting from one to the other **Addition and subtraction:** consolidate adding and subtracting any fractions by finding common denominators **Multiplication and division:** consolidate multiplying fractions by whole numbers and then multiplying fractions by fractions developing the generalisation; dividing fractions by whole numbers

References

2010 Estyn the Education and Training Inspectorate for Wales learning.wales.gov.uk

Askew, M, *How to teach fractions in KS1*, Teach Primary, UK, 2014.

Festinger, L, *A theory of cognitive dissonance*, Stanford University Press, Stanford, CA, 1957.

Gattegno, C, *For the teaching of mathematics*, vol. 1, Great Britain, Lamport, Gilbert, 1963.

Gu, L, Huang, R, & Marton, F, *Teaching with variation: An effective way of mathematics teaching in China*, World Scientific, China, 2004, pp. 309–347.

Gu, M, *Education directory Shanghai*, Shanghai Educational Press, China, 1999, p. 186.

Ross, S, *Place value: Problem solving and written assessment*, California State University, Long Beach, CA, 2002.

3

Additive reasoning

This section includes the following:

- The bar model
- Structures for addition
- Structures for subtraction
- Relationships between addition and subtraction
- Mental calculation strategies
- The progression through addition
- The progression through subtraction
- Solving problems with addition and subtraction
- Using statistics to practise addition and subtraction
- Time
- Using addition and subtraction to find differences and durations in time
- Suggested progression for teaching addition and subtraction

Introduction

Additive reasoning

> Additive reasoning is based on quantities connected by part–whole relations. Two central properties of part–whole relations involve (1) commutativity and (2) the inverse relation between addition and subtraction.
>
> (Ching) Boby Ho-Hong (2017)

The relationship between the parts and the whole is very important because it leads to an understanding of commutativity and inverse. The number sense section of this book looked at the foundations for addition and subtraction in the Early Years Foundation Stage (EYFS). For example, when exploring the number three using manipulatives, the children should be able to see that 2 add 1 equals 3, 1 add 2 equals 3, 3 subtract 2 equals 1 and 3 subtract 1 equals 2. So, they are identifying the whole, breaking it into parts and then recombining to make the whole again. At this stage, the children are being introduced to the idea of both commutativity and inverse. *Commutativity* means that it does not matter which way round the numbers are added; the sum will always be the same. *Inverse* means 'the opposite'. Addition and subtraction are inverse operations. We can use one operation to check the other.

Children need to understand that two or more parts are equal to one whole. Internalising the pattern that part add part equals whole and whole subtract part equals part will enable them to work out a full range of calculations.

The bar model

The bar model is worth discussing at this point because it is a significant visual representation that shows the links between addition and subtraction and helps children to make sense of word problems.

We have watched the practice in higher-performing jurisdictions over the last few years. One strategy that they employed in Singapore was to embed the bar model into their teaching. The bar model is a mathematical representation of a word problem. It reveals the structure of the problem and can help children 'act' out what is being asked. It is not a calculating tool, so children still need to do the arithmetic.

It is a distinctive feature of the Singapore primary mathematics curriculum, introduced to raise mathematical competences and the ability to problem solve. These were a national issue in the 1980s. It has helped dramatically improve the achievement in the mathematics of children in Singapore and has helped the country become consistently one of the top jurisdictions in the world in the TIMSS (Trends in Mathematics and Science Study).

If we are to embed bar modelling into our curriculum, we need to start using it in the EYFS. Setting very simple problems, asking the children to act them out and then demonstrating what it looks like as a bar model will familiarise them with this visual representation. The following are some examples of the types of questions we could be asking children in Year R to act out and solve.

> Freddie had three red counters and four blue counters. How many counters did Freddie have altogether?

Diagram 3.1

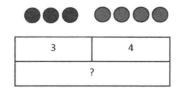

Rosie had four marbles. Alice gave her two more marbles. How many marbles does Rosie have now?

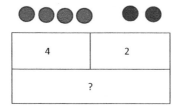

There were five pencils in the pencil pot and two rubbers. How many more pencils were there?

5	
2	?

A nursey teacher I was working with a few years ago had decided to implement the bar model with her children. She had large laminated bar models available for the children to use. These were made of 10 squares. The children began to use them by placing one object on one square. They were encouraged to count to see how many were on the bar at several points and then to count to see how many more they needed to fill it.

I observed it being used at drinks time. The teacher had some drinks to give to groups of 10 children at a time. She asked one child to take the drinks, and her job was to work out how many drinks there were and how many more were needed for the group. The teacher emphasized, for example, 'There are eight drinks, we need two more to make ten, because eight add two equals ten.'

When children move into Key Stage 1 and begin addition and subtraction, using the bar model is important so that children develop an understanding of the relationship between the two operations.

This model shows four obvious calculations.

8	11
19	

We can see that $8 + 11 = 19$, $11 + 8 = 19$, $19 - 8 = 11$ and $19 - 11 = 8$.

Adding these extra four calculations is good practice: $19 = 8 + 11$, $19 = 11 + 8$, $8 = 19 - 11$ and $11 = 19 - 8$. This reinforces the equal-to symbol as the symbol for equivalence, equal to and same as, not the answer to a calculation.

The bar model is great for missing-number problems. Using letters for the missing values is a good idea so that the children are familiar with letters replacing unknowns which is basic algebra. Algebra is specifically mentioned in Year 6; however, finding unknowns starts from Year 1. Using letters for unknowns is not advised unless the children know their letters in English. Year 2 or Year 3 might be a good time to start.

$$24 + f = 56$$

24	f
56	

From this model, we can see that to find f, we need to find the difference between 24 and 56. We could do that by counting on from 24 to 56 or back from 56 to 24. Most children find it easier to count on. They would add 6 to 24 to make 30 and then add 26 to 30 to make 56. They add 6 to 26 to make 32, which is the value of f.

Encouraging children to use a number line for counting on or back would be helpful, as shown in the following diagram.

Diagram 3.2

Counting on:

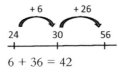

$$6 + 36 = 42$$

So, f must be 42.

Counting back:

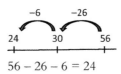

$$56 - 26 - 6 = 24$$

We have subtracted a total of 32, so $f = 42$.

$$13 + 27 = 40$$

g	
13	27

From this model, we can see that 13 and 27 are added together to give g.

$$243 - h = 145$$

243	
h	145

This model shows that to find h, we need to count on from 145 to 243 or back from 243 to 145. Either way, h is 98.

Again, a number line would be helpful for counting on or back.

Diagram 3.3

Counting on:

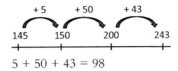

$$5 + 50 + 43 = 98$$

So, $b = 98$.

Counting back:

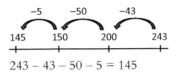

$$243 - 43 - 50 - 5 = 145$$

We have subtracted a total of 98, so b must be 98.

$24.5 + n = 39.3$

39.3	
24.5	n

Again, n can be found using a counting on or counting back strategy. We would expect children to count on 0.5 to make 25 and then 14.3 to give 39.3. Then 0.5 add 14.3 gives us n, 14.8, as shown on the following number line.

Diagram 3.4

Counting on:

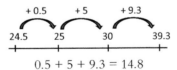

$$0.5 + 5 + 9.3 = 14.8$$

So, $n = 14.8$.

Counting back:

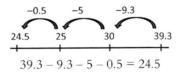

$$39.3 - 9.3 - 5 - 0.5 = 24.5$$

We have subtracted a total of 14.8, so $n = 14.8$.

We should be expecting children to use the bar model for problem solving. Here are two examples that lend themselves well to bar modelling:

■ Gemma had a collection of stamps. She gave 356 to her friend. She was left with 1780. How many stamps did Gemma start off with?

Gemma's stamps	
356	1 780

The children draw the bar and fill in the known values.

From the model, they should be able to see that they need to add the two known values to give the total number of stamps Gemma had altogether.

Now that they have this model, we could vary the problem. This can be done by varying the number of stamps that she gave to her friend, the number Gemma had left. We could also change the problem; for example, 'Gemma had 2 139 stamps, she gave 359 to her friend. How many stamps did she have left?'

Of course, when adding the variation, we should ask the children what is the same and what is different about the problem each time.

■ Sam had a collection of 576 shells. Jonny had 375 more shells. How many shells did Jonny have?

576	375
Jonny's shells	

Again, the children draw the bar model and fill in the known values.

From the model, the children can see that 576 and 375 need adding together to give the number of shells Jonny had.

After solving the problem, add variation to the question by changing the number of shells Sam had and/or the number more that Jonny had or the question to be asked; for example, how many shells did they have altogether?' Again, we could change the problem; for example, 'Sam and Jonny had a total of 1527 shells. Sam had 576 shells. How many shells did Jonny have?' Do not forget to ask the children what is the same and what is different each time you make a change!

Any of these problems can be adapted with numbers appropriate to those your children are working with.

The bar model is an important visual representation that all children need to access. Becoming fluent in using it means that they will be able to tackle more challenging problems that we would not have expected them to be able to access in the years before we were reintroduced to it.

Structures for addition

There are two structures for addition: augmentation and aggregation.

Augmentation is adding one amount on to an existing amount.

Diagram 3.5

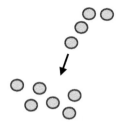

This is often more obvious when in the context of a worded scenario; for example, 'Marie had six apples. Petra gave her four more apples. How many apples does Marie have now?' Marie begins with six apples, and four more apples are added onto the six.

For augmentation, we use the vocabulary of *augend*, for the starting number; *add addend*, for the number we add and *equals sum* or *total*.

These words make a lot of sense when you look at their Latin origins. *Augend* comes from the Latin *augere*, which means 'to increase'. *Addend* comes from the Latin word *addendus*, which means 'to be added'. *Sum* comes from the Latin word *summa*, which means 'main part' or 'sum total'.

Aggregation is when two separate amounts come together.

Diagram 3.6

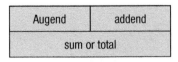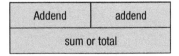

Again, this is obvious within the context of a worded scenario; for example, 'Marie had six apples. Petra had four apples. How many apples did they have altogether?' There is Marie's amount and Petra's amount, and the two are brought together and combined.

For aggregation, we use the vocabulary *addend, add addend, equals sum* or *total*.

Generally, when given calculations in Key Stage 2, the augmentation structure is used, for example, 245 + 154. We begin with 245, and we add 154 onto it.

The bar model is an excellent visual representation to show both structures.

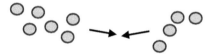

Augend	addend
sum or total	

Addend	addend
sum or total	

We need to ensure that we teach both these structures to the children when we begin teaching addition in Year 1. Giving the children simply worded scenarios to act out and answer is a good idea. Teaching the appropriate key vocabulary is also important. They pick this up easily. We introduce other words as they arise in worded scenarios.

Worded scenarios is the term I tend to use for what we would have classed as word problems in the past. A word problem should be something that cannot easily be solved; it needs an element that the children have to figure out, for example, to figure out what they need to do to find the solution. The examples used to demonstrate the structures for addition are not real problems. Children will have been working on addition and so will know to add any numbers they see which is not solving a problem. This has been the case for decades. We work on addition and then practise with some 'word problems' which are basically some numbers to add surrounded by words. I am not sure if my term is a particularly good one, but it is better than using *word problems*!

Structures for subtraction

There are two structures for subtraction. These are reduction and difference.

Reduction is as it sounds: reducing an amount or making it smaller. For example, 'Bertie had nine marbles. He gave three away. How many were left?' The children initially begin by counting out nine marbles or their own representation for marbles and then take away or subtract three. The amount left is the difference.

For this model of subtraction, we use the vocabulary *minuend*, for the number we start with; *subtract subtrahend*, the number we subtract; and *equals difference*, what is left.

Minuend comes from the Latin word *minuendus*, which means 'to diminish'. This is what happens when a number is subtracted from it. *Subtrahend* comes from the Latin word *subtrahendus*, which means 'to be taken away or removed'. *Difference* comes from the Latin word *differentia*, which means 'carrying away'.

The difference structure involves finding out how much more one quantity is than another. A strategy we use for this is counting on or back. This links well with using a number line as discussed in the sections in both number sense and numerical reasoning. Children should experience finding the difference practically. We can see from the following visual representation that the difference between 9 and 4 is 5.

Diagram 3.7

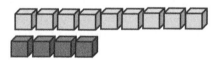

The bar model is a very helpful visual representation to show these structures.

minuend	
subtrahend	difference

As with the structures for addition, we need to ensure that we teach both to the children when we begin teaching subtraction in Year 1. Giving the children simple problems to act out and answer is a good idea.

Again, using the appropriate vocabulary is important. We need to say *subtract* as it reflects the operation. Many teachers use the words *take away*. When they do, the children may well think of food! We introduce other words, such as *take away*, as they come up in worded scenarios.

Relationships between addition and subtraction

As previously mentioned, addition and subtraction are inverse operations. We can use addition to check a subtraction, by adding the difference to the subtrahend to see if we get the minuend. We can use subtraction to check an addition, by subtracting either the augend or addend from the sum or total to see if we get the other number. One of the requirements in the national curriculum is that children check answers to a calculation using the inverse operation. I always give children calculators to check using the inverse because getting them into the habit of checking is important, but we do not want to make it laborious for them by giving them too much to calculate, particularly if it is not an operation they are focusing on in the lesson.

Addition is commutative; subtraction is not commutative. Both ideas need exploring with the children from the beginning. For example, $2 + 4 = 4 + 2$, but $6 - 2$ is not equal to $2 - 6$. Telling the children that you cannot subtract 6 from 2 is not correct because you can; the difference is -4.

Mental calculation strategies

In 1999, the National Numeracy Strategy (NSS) launched a framework for teaching mathematics. The great thing about it was that it had an emphasis on teaching mental calculation strategies. Since its demise and the introduction of the national curriculum, that emphasis has gone and most children answer calculations using written methods in Key Stage 2, even if they are not the most efficient methods. I believe we need to teach these strategies and encourage the children to think, 'Can I do this in my head, do I need jottings or is a written method more efficient?' The planning that I have written encourages teachers to start teaching mental calculation strategies in Key Stage 1. Children do not need to learn the written methods in Years 1 and 2, so this is an ideal opportunity. In Key Stage 2, they then extend, reinforce and rehearse these at the beginning of the additive reasoning unit for a few weeks. This is really paying off as children are becoming more flexible in their thinking.

We really need to expect children to use mental calculation strategies for any numbers in which no exchange is needed and for other numbers that lend themselves to a particular strategy. An expectation of the NNS was that children could add and subtract two-digit numbers mentally, using jottings by the end of Year 2. I am not sure if this expectation was widely achieved; I suspect not.

In Part 2 of the NNS document *Teaching Mental Calculation Strategies Guidance for Teachers at Key Stages 1 and 2* (1999), they discuss what mental calculation actually is:

- For many adults, mental calculation is about doing arithmetic; it involves rapid recall of number facts – knowing your number bonds to 20 and the multiplication tables to 10×10.

- Rapid recall of number facts is one aspect of mental calculation but there are others. This involves presenting children with calculations in which they have to work out the answer using known facts and not just recall it from a bank of number facts committed to memory. Children should understand and be able to use the relationship between the four operations and be able to construct equivalent calculations that help them to carry out such calculations.

The document gave these examples as an illustration:

> A year 2 child who knows that $9 + 9 = 18$ can use this to calculate mentally other results, e.g. $9 + 8, 9 + 18, 19 + 9, 19 + 19$.
> A year 4 child who knows that $6 \times 4 = 24$ can use this fact to calculate 12×4 by doubling.
> A year 6 child who knows that $36 \div 4 = 9$ can use this to calculate $56 \div 4$ by partitioning 56 into $36 + 20$ and using the knowledge of $36 \div 4$ and $20 \div 4$ to reach the answer of 14.

It is really important that we develop mathematical thinkers who can reason about which strategy they could use to answer a calculation rather than children who always use procedures. Generally, they will not be able to do this unless we teach them a bank of possibilities that they can select from.

There are several strategies that we need to encourage children to try. They are likely to have their favourite methods that work best for them, which is fine, but we need to teach a selection:

- Counting on or back
- Sequencing
- Doubles and near doubles
- Use number pairs to 1, 10, 100 and so on
- Adding/subtracting near multiples of 10 and adjusting
- Using patterns of similar calculations
- Use relationships between operations
- Using known number facts
- Bridging through 10
- Making subtraction easier (same difference, different appearance)

Counting on or back

We have discussed counting on or back as a strategy for solving problems using the bar model. Number lines are important for this. Making links to measurement is a good idea to reinforce real-life application and the measurement skills they need to learn.

For example, 'Jodie had £24, her mum gave her another £13. How much money does she have now?'

The children would mark £24 on a number line and then add £6 and then £7 or add £10 and then £3.

Diagram 3.8

This strategy is a great one for finding time differences and durations. For example, 'Flo went for a bike ride. She set off from home at 10:35 and got home again at 13:50. For how long was she out on her ride?'

Diagram 3.9

From this model, we can see that Flo was out on her ride for 3 hours 15 minutes.

Here is an example of how Year 1 children were finding the difference using the context of length. They first had to have some practice at drawing lines with a ruler. Once they had drawn a selection of lines, they had to identify the longest and shortest and find the difference between them.

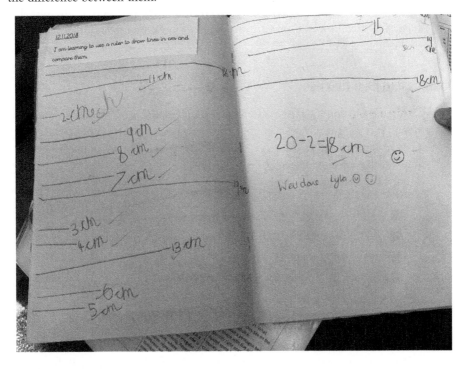

Sequencing

Sequencing is a strategy in which one number is kept the same, the other is partitioned and each part added.

For example,

- $24 + 14 = 24 + 10 + 4 = 34 + 4 = 38$
- $258 + 136 = 258 + 100 + 30 + 6 = 388 + 2 + 4 = 394$
- $35.2 + 21.4 = 35.2 + 20 + 1 + 0.4 = 56.6$
- $78 - 43 = 78 - 40 - 3 = 38 - 3 = 35$
- $384 - 257 = 384 - 200 - 50 - 7 = 134 - 4 - 3 = 127$
- $78.6 - 32.4 = 78.6 - 30 - 2 - 0.4$

It is important that we teach this practically using manipulatives, such as Dienes equipment, so that the children understand what is happening. For example, if adding 24 and 13, they make both numbers. They take the one 10 from the 13 and place it with the 24, so making 34. They then add the three 1s making a sum of 37.

Again, practising this within measurement is helpful. For example, 'Jo had a piece of string which was 96 cm in length. He cut off 32 cm and gave it to his friend. How much did he have left?' The calculation would look like this: 96 cm – 30c m = 66 cm; 66 cm – 2 cm = 64 cm.

We would expect children to keep 96 cm whole and partition 32 cm into 30 cm and 2 cm. They then subtract 30 cm from 96 cm to give 66 cm and then subtract 2 cm to give a difference of 64 cm.

Doubles and near doubles

Children begin doubling in Year R. So continuing doubling throughout Key Stage 1, even though it is not specifically mentioned in the national curriculum, makes sense. Including near doubles also makes sense. Near doubling is a strategy which works for adding numbers that are close to each other.

For example,

- $25 + 26$, double 25 and add one
- $150 + 160$, double 150 and add ten
- $0.6 + 0.7$, double 0.6 and add 0.1
- $2560 + 2570$, double 2500 and add 130

As always, begin practically using Dienes or similar representations so that the children understand what is happening. For example, if exploring $6 + 5$, they make 6 and 5, take 5 from the 6, so doubling the 5 to make 10 and then add another 1.

They practise within the context of measurement. For example, 'Bobbie had £2.50. His friend had £2.60. How much did they have in total?' The children should be able to see that £2.50 and £2.60 are close together, so they can double £2.50 and add on another 10 pence to give a sum or total of £5.10.

Use number pairs to 1, 10, 100 and so on

Children need to know their number pairs for all numbers to 10. They begin exploring these in Year R. By Year 1, they should be able to recall them quickly, particularly those for 10. Often, teachers say that many of their children do not have instant recall of these facts. I think one reason could be that the children are expected to recall the facts but do not apply them in other situations frequently enough. As shown later, various mental calculation strategies require that children use their number pairs for 10, for example, the making 10 and making a subtraction-easier strategies.

Tens frames are a good resource for practicing number pairs for 10. The children place 10 double-sided counters on a tens frame. They turn one double-sided counter over at a time to make number bonds for 10. As they do this, they write the appropriate number statements and draw circle and bar models to show what they have made. The following is an example.

Diagram 3.10

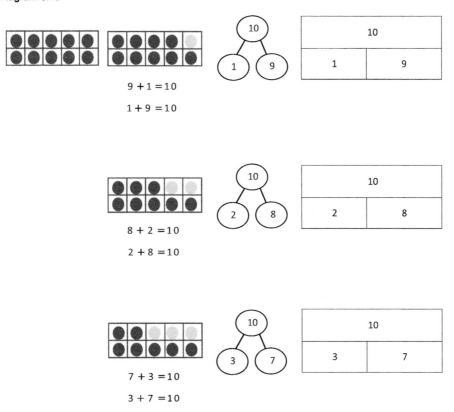

$$9 + 1 = 10$$
$$1 + 9 = 10$$

$$8 + 2 = 10$$
$$2 + 8 = 10$$

$$7 + 3 = 10$$
$$3 + 7 = 10$$

As they get older, they will use their number pairs for ten to derive facts for other numbers such as 20, 100 and 1. For example, if they know that 2 add 8 equals 10, they know that 12 add 8 equals 20, that 20 add 80 equals 100 and that 0.2 add 0.8 equals 1.

For example,

- $13 + 17 = 20 + 10 = 30$
- $54 + 46 = 90 + 10 = 100$
- $258 + 142 = 300 + 90 + 10 = 300 + 100$
- $24.9 + 34.1 = 50 + 7 + 1 = 58$
- $13.56 + 12.44 = 20 + 5 + 0.9 + 0.1 = 25 + 1 = 26$

We should give children calculations and worded scenarios that involve adding numbers that make 10 so that they can make use of these facts and therefore reinforce and consolidate them.

As always, we need to begin practically. The children make two numbers using Dienes equipment or similar, they add the 10s and then the 1s, exchanging the ten 1s for a 10. For example, $16 + 14$.

Diagram 3.11

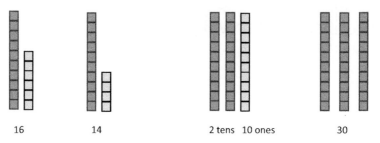

| 16 | 14 | 2 tens 10 ones | 30 |

Give children worded scenarios within the context of measurement. For example, using representations for pounds, children could answer scenarios similar to the following:

- Bertie had £24. Suzie had £26? How much money did they have altogether?

As with the calculation example, the children add the 10s and then the 1s, they exchange ten £1 coins for £10 to give £50.

Using number pairs for subtraction is also important. If children know that, for example, $7 + 3 = 10$, they should know that $10 - 7 = 3$ and $10 - 3 = 7$. Therefore, if subtracting 7 from 20, the answer will be 13, and if subtracting 17 from 40, the answer will be 23. We need to give children the opportunity to practise this as well.

Adding/subtracting near multiples of 10 and adjusting

In the days of the NNS, adding and subtracting near multiples of 10 and adjusting was a popular mental calculation strategy. Nine is close to 10, so if adding a number that ends with 9, we can round up to the next multiple of 10 and adjust by subtracting 1 because we have added one too many. If subtracting a number ending with nine, we can subtract the next multiple of 10 and add an extra one because we have subtracted one too many.

For example, if adding 39 to 56, we would add 40 and then subtract 1 to give 95. Using manipulatives so that children can physically do this is important.

Diagram 3.12

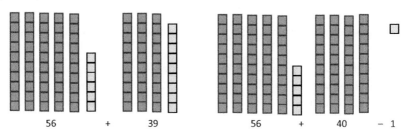

$$56 \quad + \quad 39 \qquad\qquad 56 \quad + \quad 40 \quad - \quad 1$$

This strategy works for adding any numbers; for example, if adding 42 to 124, we add 40 and then another 2. If we subtract 48 from 87, we can subtract 50 and then add 2 because we have subtracted two too many. We have to be careful how we adjust!

We should give the children opportunities to practise this skill.

1	2	3	4	5	6	7	8	9	10
11	12	13	14	15	16	17	18	19	20
21	22	23	24	25	26	27	28	29	30
31	32	33	34	35	36	37	38	39	40
41	42	43	44	45	46	47	48	49	50
51	52	53	54	55	56	57	58	59	60
61	62	63	64	65	66	67	68	69	70
71	72	73	74	75	76	77	78	79	80
81	82	83	84	85	86	87	88	89	90
91	92	93	94	95	96	97	98	99	100

Asking children to take their finger for a walk around a 100 square is fun.

Give a list of instructions; for example, 'Put your finger on the number 4, add 10, add 9, add 12, add 18 and subtract 9. What number have you landed on?' You can do this with children of any age; this activity is differentiated by the numbers you ask children to add and subtract and the speed at which you go.

When using a 100 square and asked to add 10, often young children will count in 1s along the rows. This is probably because they have not explored the patterns on a 100 square sufficiently. Ask them to add 10 to 5 and then keep asking them to add 10, with everyone counting in ones. On a classroom 100 square, circle the numbers landed on. Keep going until reaching 85 and then ask the children what they notice. Do they have to keep counting 10 individual numbers, or is there a quicker way? They should notice that they are simply dropping down a row, the 10s number increases by one each time and the 1s number stays the same.

Children need to practically explore adding 9. For example, they make 24 and 9. They line the nine 1s up alongside a 10 to show that 9 is one less than 10. Then they add the 10 to 24 to make 34 and subtract 1.

Age-appropriate worded scenarios could include examples such as these:

- Sophie had 35 marbles. Her mum gave her 19 more. How many marbles does Sophie have now?
  The children add 20 to 35, to give 55, and then subtract 1. Sophie now has 54 marbles.

- Bertie scored 354 points on a computer game. Sam scored 99 points more. How many points did Sam score?
  The children add 100 and subtract 1 to give 453.

- Tom had a collection of 163 football cards. He gave 49 cards to his friend. How many did he have left?
  The children would subtract 50 and then add 1. Tom had 114 left.

Using patterns of similar calculations

This is similar to variation. If children know that $6 + 7 = 13$, they should be able to tell you other facts; for example,

- $6 + 8 = 14$; because 8 is one more than 7, the answer must be one more than 13.
- $7 + 8 = 15$; because 7 is one more than 6, the answer must be one more than 14.

They should be able to make up a lot of other facts without working them out because of what they notice and the patterns they see. We do not give the children enough opportunities to think like this, so they tend to calculate everything when they could just look for patterns.

Use relationships between operations

Understanding commutativity and inverse are really important. If the children really understand these concepts, they will be able to use them to make simple mental calculations. For example, if they know that 14 add 6 equals 20, they should be able to use that to work out the answer to 20 subtract 14. They also should be able to check using their knowledge of number pairs.

Children seeing the links between repeated addition and multiplication ($4 \times 3 = 4 + 4 + 4 = 12$) and repeated subtraction and division ($12 - 4 - 4 - 4 = 3$ groups of 4) is important. Sometimes these relationships get lost towards the end of Key Stage 2 when children use written methods for the four operations.

Using known number facts

We all want our children to become flexible thinkers. Unfortunately, the current emphasis on written methods means that often we do not allow for time to develop children's flexibility in thinking. Using known number facts to derive others is a great way to do this. Writing a fact on the board and asking children to write down as many other facts as they can in about three minutes is a good idea. Encouraging them to add, subtract, double and halve, multiply and divide by powers of 10 enables children to think, reason and develop flexibility.

For example,

If I know that $9 + 8 = 17$, I also know that . . .

- $19 + 8 = 27$ (adding 10 to 9 means that we need to add 10 to the sum)
- $38 + 16 = 54$ (doubling 19 and 8 means that we need to double 27)
- $8 + 9 = 17$ (commutativity)
- $17 - 8 = 9$ (inverse operation)
- $27 - 8 = 19$ (adding 10 to 17 means that we add 10 to the 9)
- $1.9 + 0.8 = 2.7$ (dividing both numbers by 10 means that we need to divide the sum by 10)
- $190 + 80 = 270$ (multiplying both numbers by 10 means that we need to multiply the sum by 10)

Bridging through 10

The NNS introduced many teachers to the concept of bridging ten. When we add numbers together, we can partition them in different ways to make the operation easy. We can also take numbers from one amount and give them to another, and we will get the same sum.

Bridging through 10 involves making a number a multiple of 10. For example, $54 + 38$ could become $60 + 32$ by taking 6 from 38 and adding it to 54. We could also take 2 from 54 and add it to 38 to make the calculation $52 + 40$. Both new calculations are much easier to answer.

Again, initially, this needs to be carried out practically using manipulatives such as Dienes equipment.

Diagram 3.13

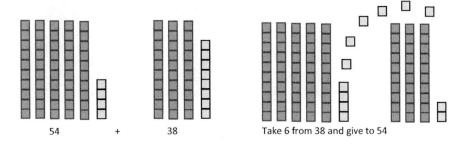

| 54 | + | 38 | Take 6 from 38 and give to 54 |

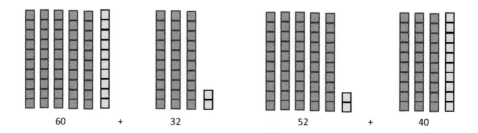

$$60 \quad + \quad 32 \qquad 52 \quad + \quad 40$$

Once children have an understanding of this strategy, they can then adapt it for other calculations which involve bridging 1, 100, 1000 and so on

Here are some examples:

- 256 + 179 could become 255 + 180, which then could become 235 + 200, which is equivalent to 435.
- 27.6 + 15.7 could become 28 + 15.3, which could then become 30 + 13.3, which is equivalent to 43.3.
- 4368 + 2875 could become 4363 + 2880, which could become 4343 + 2900, which could then become 4243 + 3000, which is equivalent to 7243.

Making subtraction easier

Making a subtraction easier is a great mental calculation strategy. This strategy was not brought to us by the NNS; a friend showed it to me years ago. It probably has an official name, maybe same difference, different calculation, but I find that it does make subtraction simpler and so have used that term. To begin teaching this strategy, it is important that children understand that subtracting different combinations of numbers can have the same difference. I always start this with cubes. The children make two towers, one of four cubes and one of six.

Diagram 3.14

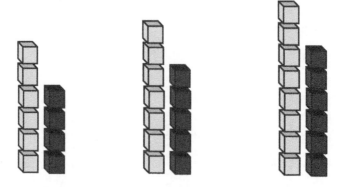

They can clearly see that there is a difference of two. They can make the calculation 6 − 4 = 2.

They then add another cube to each tower to make $7 - 5 = 2$. The difference remains the same. They then add another cube to each tower to make $8 - 6 = 2$. The difference remains the same. We keep doing this so that they understand that if we add the same amount to each number, the difference will always be the same. We then start to calculate. The aim is to turn the subtrahend into a multiple of 10, which makes the subtraction easier. After children practise like this, they then move on to make 1 and 100s. Here are some examples:

- $67 - 48 = 69 - 50 = 19$ (by adding two onto both numbers)
- $343 - 175 = 348 - 180 = 368 - 200 = 168$ (by adding 5 and then 20 onto both numbers)
- $5658 - 2869 = 5659 - 2870 = 5689 - 2900 = 5789 - 3000 = 2789$ (by adding 1, 30 and then 100 onto both numbers)
- $24.62 - 15.74 = 24.68 - 15.8 = 24.88 - 16 = 28.88 - 20 = 8.88$ (by adding 0.06, 0.2 and then 4 onto both numbers)

The children really enjoy this strategy! So it is worth teaching.

The 2018 Standard Assessment Test Paper for arithmetic in Year 6 had a few questions which could have been answered quickly and efficiently using mental calculation strategies; for example,

$$56.38 + 24.7 =$$

For this calculation, the children could have used the bridging 10 strategy to give the calculation $56.08 + 25$, taking 0.3 from 56.38 and adding it to 24.7, which is a simpler calculation.

$$\boxed{} - 10 = 298$$

For this calculation, children could have used their knowledge of inverse. They could also have reasoned that the minuend must be 10 more than 298 so that when 10 is subtracted, the difference will be 298.

$$\boxed{} = 5{,}776 - 855$$

For this calculation, the children could have used the making subtraction easier strategy to give the calculation $5\,781 - 860$ and then $5\,821 - 900$ and $5\,921 - 1\,000$ to make $4\,921$.

$$10 - 5.4 =$$

Children could have used the bridging-10 strategy for this calculation by taking 0.6 from 10 and adding it to 5.4 to give the calculation $9.4 - 6$.

$$6 - 5.738 =$$

Children could have used a counting-on strategy for this calculation and added 0.002, 0.06 and 0.2 to get to 6, giving a difference of 0.262.

Most children resorted to written methods for all calculations that they could not solve mentally. The most likely reason for this is that they did not consider other strategies because they have not been taught how to use them.

The main message in this part of the book is that children should use mental calculation strategies as often as possible and not use standard written methods for the four operations unless a mental calculation strategy cannot be easily used or a written method is more efficient or quicker.

The progression through addition

When beginning to teach written methods to the children, we should begin by showing a series of addition calculations and discuss which methods would be best to use. By this time, they will have spent a few weeks revisiting mental calculation strategies learned in previous years and so will be in a position to make sensible decisions.

For example,

- 125 + 126 (near doubles)
- 346 + 223 (sequencing)
- 225 + 199 (making 10 or rounding and adjusting)
- 627 + 373 (number pairs to 10 and 100)
- 445 +187 (making 10 and 100)
- 3537 + 2986 (the written method because several exchanges are needed)

When teaching the written method for addition, introducing them when there is an exchange needed is important. Calculations with no exchange should be carried out using a mental calculation strategy. If we start teaching the written method in Year 3 when it is not necessary, this gives the message that a written method is the one children need to use from now.

Of course, all the way through their learning of addition, children need to estimate the sum and check using subtraction with a calculator. They should also become increasingly familiar with the vocabulary of *augend add addend* and *equals sum or total*.

Using manipulatives is vital to ensure that children really understand what they are doing when they calculate. Manipulatives are needed to enable the children to make sense of the arithmetic they are carrying out. They increase children's engagement and enjoyment and develop visual images and understanding. They help children work together in pairs or small groups and share ideas. They are tools to help children solve problems, investigate patterns and relationships and demonstrate results and reasoning. Most importantly, they provide a bridge to abstract thinking, and they help you to assess what the children understand.

In Year 1, the national curriculum expects children to add one-digit and two-digit numbers to 20. This really is not much of a progression from Year R, when they should be exploring different ways to make all the numbers to 10, which is the early stage of addition, so I would increase that to 50 or maybe 100 if children are ready. I would give numbers that do not require an exchange.

Children need to move on from counting everything one at a time. Resources such as Numicon are ideal for this.

Diagram 3.15

If adding 6 and 9, children use the appropriate Numicon plates and put them together. They should be able to see that the sum is going to be greater than 10, so they place the 10 plate over 10 holes and see what is left. This is the bridging-10 mental calculation strategy.

Year 1 could use Numicon to add greater numbers such as 12 and 27.

Diagram 3.16

They would add the 10s first and then the 1s to give a sum of 39. This is the sequencing mental calculation strategy.

In Year 2, the expectation is that children use manipulatives, visual representations and mental skills to add two-digit numbers and 1s, two-digit numbers and 10s, two two-digit numbers and three one-digit numbers. It suggests in the notes and guidance of the national curriculum that children begin recording their addition calculations in columns so that they will be ready for formal written methods in Year 3.

Teaching them about exchanging is necessary. Dienes is a useful manipulative for adding larger numbers, for example, 36 + 28.

Diagram 3.17

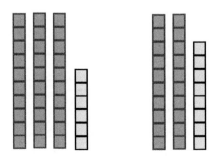

Bridging 10 is a good strategy for teaching for this. It reinforces number pairs to 10. The children add the 10s together first. Then they bridge 10 by taking 4 from the eight 1s to add to the 6. They exchange the ten 1s for a 10 rod and make the sum of 64.

Diagram 3.18

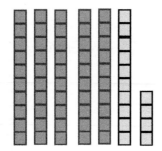 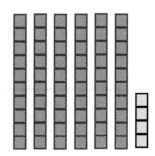

Towards the end of a unit on addition, Year 2 children could follow the suggestions in the notes and guidance and start recording as follows:

$$
\begin{array}{r}
36 \\
+\ 28 \\
\hline
50 \\
+\ 14 \\
\hline
64 \\
\end{array}
$$

This is called the expanded method because the 10s are added and the result is recorded; then the 1s are added and the result recorded underneath the 10s. Finally, the two results are added to give the sum. Children should continue to use manipulatives as they explore this way of recording. This way of recording prepares them for Year 3.

Putting addition practically into the context of measurement, for example, pence, whole pounds and centimetres, is helpful.

All the way through Key Stage 2, children should be given the opportunity to explore addition using manipulatives. For larger numbers, using place-value counters is better.

In Year 3, the new learning is to add three-digit numbers. Variation suggests that we should just make a one-step change. So, beginning with using the expanded written method started at the end of Year 2 but for three-digit numbers with one exchange is helpful. For example, 236 + 128:

$$
\begin{array}{r}
236 \\
+\ 128 \\
\hline
300 \\
50 \\
+\ \ \ 14 \\
\hline
364 \\
\end{array}
$$

The children will have been used to starting with the most significant digits first all the way through Key Stage 1, so we begin with this. After some practice at this, we then explore what happens when missing the middle part and going towards the short-written method. I always use the examples worked on initially and make the mistake of starting with the most significant digits:

$$236$$
$$+\ 128$$
$$3514$$

This is clearly incorrect because the answer should be 364. I ask the children what I have done wrong. This is a good way to check their understanding of place value. Most children can tell me that I should have exchanged the ten 1s when adding 6 and 8 for a 10 and added that to the 10s digits: the 3 and the 2. We then talk about how they could approach this to make it correct and reach the conclusion that we could start with the least significant digit (the 1s):

$$236$$
$$+\ 128$$
$$364$$

We always begin with an exchange from 1s to 10s, then 10s to 100s and finally a mixture in which two exchanges are needed.

I always link addition to measurement because the children have worked on tenths in place value, so we can add centimetre and millimetre lengths using centimetre notation. For example, they measure two lengths of paper or string and find the total length. In this way, children learn that adding decimal numbers together is the same process as adding whole numbers. I usually demonstrate this with examples that are one tenth of the size as examples previously worked on:

$$23.6\ \mathrm{cm}$$
$$+\ 12.8\ \mathrm{cm}$$
$$36.4\ \mathrm{cm}$$

In Year 4, the children extend what they have done in Year 3 to adding four-digit numbers. Again, making links to adding numbers with two decimal places within the context of length in metres and centimetres using metre notation is important. They measure different lengths and find totals of two or more.

By the time children reach the end of Year 4, they should have mastered the process of the short-written method for addition.

In Year 5, they should be able to add larger numbers and those with three-decimal places within the context of length, mass, capacity and volume. We should not need to teach the process of addition in Year 5; children should have mastered it. They should be focusing on problem solving with both addition and subtraction. However, I was talking to a Year 5 teacher recently who told me that she still had to teach these processes to her class because they were not able to do the basic calculations of addition and subtraction. This tells me that in earlier years, enough time had not been spent teaching, practising and consolidating this area of mathematics.

The progression through subtraction

As mentioned in the progression through addition, when beginning to teach written methods to children, we need to begin by showing a series of subtraction calculations and discuss which methods would be best to use.

For example,

■ 120 – 60 (halving)

■ 346 – 134 (sequencing)

■ 225 – 199 (making subtraction easier or rounding and adjusting)

■ 654 – 278 (making subtraction easier)

■ 307 – 299 (counting on)

■ 3537 – 2986 (the written method because several exchanges are needed)

As with addition, when teaching the written method for subtraction, introducing them when an exchange is needed is important.

Of course, all the way through their learning of subtraction, children need to estimate the difference and check using addition with a calculator. They should also become increasingly familiar with the vocabulary of *minuend subtract subtrahend* and *equals difference*.

In Year 1, the national curriculum expects children to subtract one-digit and two-digit numbers to 20. As with addition, I would increase this to 50 or maybe 100 if they are ready.

Resources such as Numicon are ideal for this. For example, 15 – 9. Children make 15 using Numicon. They cover with a 9 plate and can see that they have 6 remaining.

Diagram 3.19

Year 1 could use Numicon to subtract greater numbers such as 36 and 15 without exchange.

Diagram 3.20

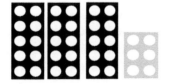
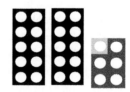

They would subtract 10 first to give 26 and then cover the 6 with a 5 plate to leave 1. They should be able to tell you that the difference is 21.

In Year 2, the expectation is that children use manipulatives, visual representations and mental skills to subtract two-digit numbers and 1s, two-digit numbers and 10s and two two-digit numbers.

Continuing to teach them about exchange is necessary, as they will now be ready to exchange for subtraction. Dienes is a useful manipulative for subtracting larger numbers, for example, 54–38.

Diagram 3.21

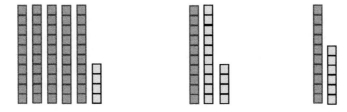

They first subtract three 10s. Then they need to subtract eight 1s, but there are not enough, so they need to exchange one 10 for ten 1s. They will have fourteen 1s and can now subtract 8 to give a difference of 16.

Throughout Key Stage 2, children should use manipulatives to explore subtraction of increasingly greater numbers. As with addition, place-value counters are a good resource.

In Year 3, the new learning is to subtract three-digit numbers. They have begun to work with the least significant digits first for addition, so dealing with the least significant digits first for subtraction straight away makes sense.

We always begin with an exchange from 1s to 10s, then 10s to 100s and finally a mixture where there are two exchanges needed.

$$2^2 \cancel{3}^1 6$$
$$-1\ 2\ 8$$
$$\overline{1\ 0\ 8}$$

Linking subtraction to measurement and numbers with one decimal place is sensible. For example, they measure two lengths of paper or string and find the difference between them. In this way, children learn that subtracting decimal numbers is the same process as subtracting whole numbers. I usually demonstrate this with examples that are one tenth of the size as examples previously worked on:

$$2^2 \cancel{3}.^1 6 \text{ cm}$$
$$-1\ 2\ .\ 8 \text{ cm}$$
$$\overline{1\ 0\ .\ 8 \text{ cm}}$$

By the time children reach Year 4, they should have mastered the short-written method for subtraction. They extend what they have done in Year 3 to subtracting four-digit numbers. Again, making links to subtracting numbers with two decimal places within the context of length in metres and centimetres using metre notation is important. They measure different lengths and find differences between pairs of lengths.

In Year 5, they should be able to subtract larger numbers and those with three-decimal places within the context of length, mass, capacity and volume. As with addition, there should be no need to teach this; children should have mastered this by now.

Solving problems with addition and subtraction

When the children have mastered the processes for addition and subtraction, they can work on real word problems instead of worded scenarios! Word problems should be set so that the children have to think about what they need to do to find a solution. So, mixing the two operations and asking problems that require both operations are helpful. When creating or selecting word problems, we need to create, or look for, those that use vocabulary such as *take away*, *more*, *less*, *altogether* and *minus*. This is essential for broadening their ability to solve a variety of problems. Expect children to draw the bar model discussed earlier. They add known values and deduce which is the missing value so that they can visualise what they need to do to find the answer.

Problems could include the following:

- Stacy had £8.70. Adam had £6.85. How much money did they have altogether? How much more money did Stacy have?

- Will ran 755 m in two minutes. Adam ran 980 m in two minutes. How far did they run altogether? How much farther did Adam run?

- Katie drew a line 15.7 cm in length. Ruby drew a line of 12.8 cm long. What was the total length of the two lines? How much longer was Katie's line?

- The volume of water left in Cindy's bottle was 0.785 l. The volume left in Maggie's bottle was 1.23 l. How much more water was in Maggie's bottle? What is the total volume left in the two bottles?

- Nathan saved £250.35, and he was given £135.50 for his birthday. He wanted to spend £425.99 on a PlayStation. How much more money does he need?

- James used some of his savings to buy a remote-control car. It cost £145.30. After he bought it, he had £79.56 left. How much money did he start off with?

These types of problem can be asked of all children, provided the numbers and contexts are adapted so they are appropriate for a particular year group. Also, do not forget to add variation!

Using statistics to practise addition and subtraction

The national curriculum requires us to teach statistics from Year 2 to Year 6. I would include simple pictograms and tally charts in Year 1. I am not sure why the decision was made to take statistics out of Year 1; it always used to be there! In good Early Years settings, children use Venn and Carroll diagrams for sorting; they are also often introduced to tallying and simple pictograms, so many children will be familiar with them. Venn and Carroll diagrams are not included in the national curriculum anymore but are really useful for sorting, for example, shapes, odd and even numbers, so I would encourage teachers to continue to use these.

Following are the national curriculum requirements:

Year 2

- interpret and construct simple pictograms, tally charts, block diagrams and simple tables
- ask and answer simple questions by counting the number of objects in each category and sorting the categories by quantity
- ask and answer questions about totalling and comparing categorical data

Year 3

- interpret and present data using bar charts, pictograms and tables
- solve one-step and two-step questions [for example, 'How many more?' and 'How many fewer?'] using information presented in scaled bar charts and pictograms and tables

Year 4

- interpret and present discrete and continuous data using appropriate graphical methods, including bar charts and time graphs
- solve comparison, sum and difference problems using information presented in bar charts, pictograms, tables and other graphs

Year 5

- solve comparison, sum and difference problems using information presented in a line graph
- complete, read and interpret information in tables, including timetables

Year 6

- interpret and construct pie charts and line graphs and use these to solve problems
- calculate and interpret the mean as an average

From Years 2 to 5, children are expected to ask and answer questions or solve problems that involve finding sums and differences. Therefore, including statistics as part of any practice activities involved in a unit on addition and subtraction makes perfect sense. Within this, we need to be teaching statistical skills as and when they arise. We should present a variety of graphs for children to interpret. We should then ask children questions that involve finding sums and differences, encouraging them to use mental calculation strategies whenever these are more efficient than written methods. Children need to devise their own graphs from data they collect and from data given to them and ask and answer questions based on their findings.

The following are some ideas based on the planning we use in some schools that show how we make links with statistics, addition and subtraction in each year group. These could form the basis of a series of lessons.

In Year 2, we could show a tally chart similar to the following one.

Packed lunches	⊦⊦⊤1 ⊦⊦⊤1 ⊦⊦⊤1 ⊦⊦⊤1 I I I I
School dinners	⊦⊦⊤1 ⊦⊦⊤1 ⊦⊦⊤1 ⊦⊦⊤1 ⊦⊦⊤1 ⊦⊦⊤1 I I
Go home	⊦⊦⊦1 I I I

We could then ask children to tell you what it is all about. Agree that it shows what children do at lunchtime. Suggest that it might be helpful if there was a title. Together, make one up. What does each mark represent? What about the diagonal lines? Ask, for example, how many have school dinners, how many more have packed lunch than go home, how many fewer go home than have school dinner and what is the difference between the number who have packed lunches and school dinners? They answer the questions by finding the information on the chart and using the mental calculation strategies they have learned.

Make up a tally to show what your class do at lunchtime and ask questions similar to those presented earlier.

Make a tally for favourite pets. Ask children to draw this on plain paper. They then make up some of their own questions similar to those you modelled. Ask them to make up one of each type: how many, how many more, how many fewer, what is the difference? They then give them to a friend to answer them.

We can then extend this by turning a tally chart into a frequency table in which the children record the numbers represented by the tallies. In the following example, children would add 17 to the right-hand column for Spain, 3 for Tobago, 16 for Greece and so on.

Spain	⊥┼┤ ⊥┼┤ ⊥┼┤ | |	
Tobago	| | |	
Greece	⊥┼┤ ⊥┼┤ ⊥┼┤ |	
South Africa	⊥┼┤	
Australia	| | | |	
Iceland	┼┼┤ | | | |	
France	⊥┼┤ ⊥┼┤ ⊥┼┤	
Italy	⊥┼┤ ⊥┼┤ |	

Tell the children this is a tally of the holidays booked last week at a travel agent. Discuss the countries and locate them on a map. Ask the children to count the tallies and tell you the totals for each country. Add these to the third column. Tell them that you have created a table which is a way of representing information using numbers. Ask questions as described earlier for the tally chart.

Draw up another set of tally marks for the same information or similar and ask the children to turn it into a table. Stress that they need to write the countries and the headings 'country' and 'number of people'. Model this first. Once they have created their table, they make up their own questions as before for a friend to answer. Then they turn their table into a bar chart.

You could then spend some time on pictograms. Show a pictogram similar to the one below where one symbol represents one item.

Diagram 3.22

Skirts	☺ ☺ ☺ ☺ ☺ ☺ ☺ ☺
Trousers	☺ ☺ ☺ ☺ ☺ ☺ ☺
Dresses	☺ ☺ ☺ ☺
Coats	☺ ☺ ☺ ☺ ☺ ☺
Skirts	☺ ☺ ☺
Shorts	☺ ☺ ☺ ☺ ☺ ☺ ☺ ☺ ☺ ☺ ☺ ☺
Jumpers	☺ ☺

Ask children if they know what this is. Agree it is called a pictogram. Make up what it might show, for example, favourite items of clothing or what is in the sale at a clothes shop. Discuss similarities and differences between this and the tally and bar charts. Agree that it is a little like a tally, but point out that instead of lines, symbols represent each one. As before, ask questions from this pictogram.

Give the children the opportunity to create their own with as much guidance as they need. Once they have, they make up and answer their own questions.

Display this pictogram or one where each symbol represents two. Tell the children that it shows the number of animals a wild-life expert saw in the jungle.

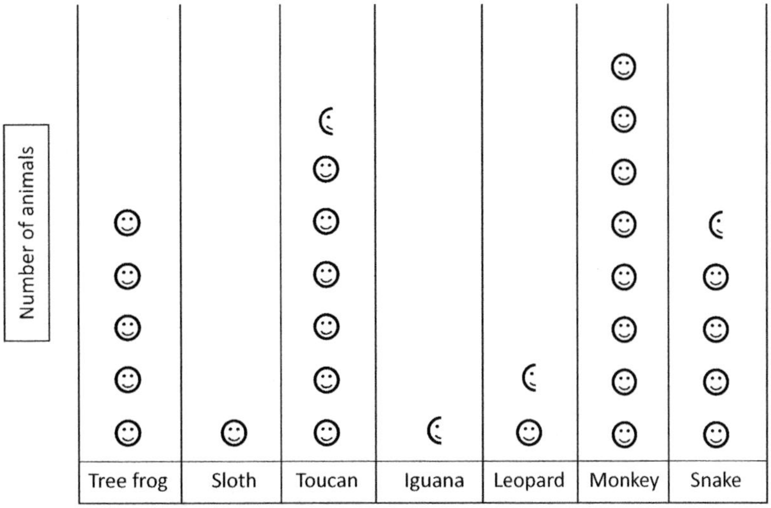

	Tree frog	Sloth	Toucan	Iguana	Leopard	Monkey	Snake

How is this pictogram different from and how is it the same as the previous one? Agree that it uses symbols; the difference is that there are some half symbols. What does this mean? Agree that each symbol cannot stand for one animal because there is no such thing as half a living animal. Can the children figure out that each symbol must represent two animals or any multiple of two? Ask questions as before and then ask the children to make four statements that involve addition and subtraction. Next, ask the children to display the information using both a tally and a table.

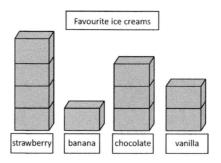

You could introduce block diagrams using towers of cubes in Year R or Year 1. Use the favourite ice creams idea. Give the children a choice of pink cubes for strawberry, yellow for banana, brown for chocolate and white for vanilla. They each pick one to show their preferred flavour out of the four. Together, make towers of the same colour. Discuss results, including which is the most/least popular. Ask questions as before. Then ask the children to draw what they see. Guide them in labelling: flavours, number of children and a title. As before, they make statements from their diagrams that involve addition and subtraction.

These ideas can be adapted for use in Year 2 and added to a unit on addition and subtraction.

In Year 3, you could begin by choosing a theme, for example, favourite animals or pets. Together, make a list of about six. Ask the children to choose their favourite. Make a tally of their choices and then turn the tally into a table. Ask questions that involve 'How many altogether . . .?' 'How many more . . .?' 'How many fewer . . .?' and 'What is the difference between . . .?' The children use mental calculation strategies to add and subtract to answer your questions.

Next ask the children to choose a topic. Together, make a list and tally. The children then turn the tally into a table and think of some questions to ask using 'How many . . . altogether?' 'How many more . . .?' 'How many fewer . . .?' and 'What is the difference between . . .?' as guides. Invite children to ask their questions and the class to answer.

The children could then work with a partner to choose their own idea and collect the information, represent it and ask questions as before.

Show the children a pictogram, such as the following example.

Diagram 3.23

Ways of coming to school	Number of children
Car	☆☆☆☆☆☆ ☆☆
Bus	☆☆☆☆☆
Walk	☆☆☆☆☆ ☆☆☆☆☆
Taxi	☆
Bicycle	☆☆☆☆

Ask 'How many altogether . . .?' 'How many more/fewer . . .?' and 'What is the difference type questions . . .?' Tell the children that each star represents two children and ask them the questions again. Repeat for symbols representing three, four and five, encouraging the children to count in steps of each multiple.

Ask the children to make up their own pictogram for something that interests them. They can make up their own data and choose how many their symbol represents. They make up and answer their own questions as you modelled.

Show another pictogram, such as the one that follows, in which there are half symbols:

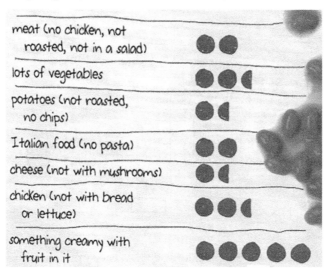

Ask the children what the symbols could stand for. Establish any even number. Ask the same type of questions as previously, when one symbol represents 2, then 4 and 6.

The children then make up their own examples with half symbols and make up and answer their own questions.

Show children a bar chart similar to the one that follows:

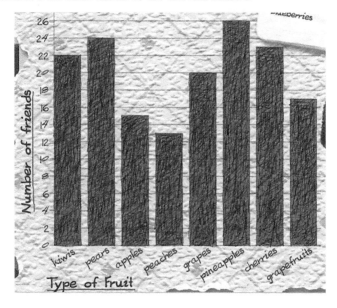

Ask children how this is the same as and different from a pictogram. Agree that both show data, but point out that they represent the data in a different way: one uses symbols and the other bars. Discuss how to read information from the bar chart.

Ask questions about this chart in the same way as before so that they can use mental calculation strategies for addition and subtraction to answer them.

You could then ask them to change the pictograms they made previously to bar charts and make up different questions to ask and answer.

Diagram 3.24

Show a bar chart similar to this to the children. What do they notice?

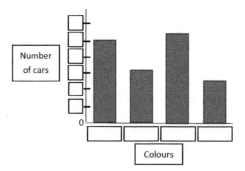

Can they identify the missing information? What do they think they need to do to it to make it useful? Give children a copy and ask them to add their own information and to remember to give it a title. Encourage them to use a scale that increases in 2s, 4s and/or 6s because some of the values are halfway between the divisions.

Once they have completed it, the children work with a partner to make up and answer each other's questions.

In Year 4, the children could revisit tallies, tables, pictograms and bar charts from Year 3. They then need to explore time graphs.

Show a simple time graph, such as the one that follows.

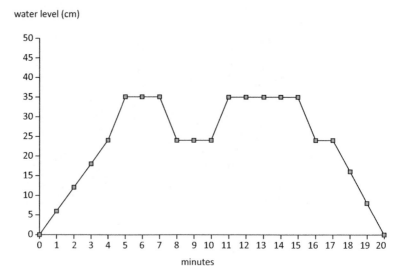

Graphs like this can be found on the NNS's interactive teaching programme (ITP) 'line graph'. Ask the children to tell you what it shows. Agree that it shows the water level, possibly in a bath, over a 20-minute period. Ask the children to make up a story that would go with the graph.

Next ask questions that involve totals and differences for children to answer using mental calculation strategies; for example, 'What is the difference between the water level at 5 minutes and that at 19 minutes?'

You could ask children to make up their own information on this theme, create a time graph and then make up their own questions to ask and answer.

The following time graph shows a lorry driver's journey. Again, this is from the NSS's ITP 'line graph'.

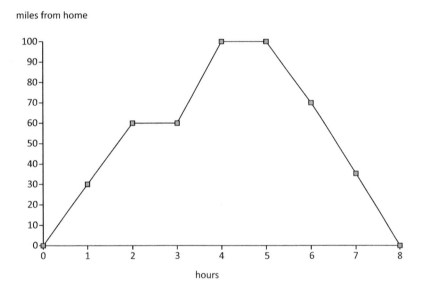

Can the children tell you what it shows? Agree that it is the distance the lorry driver travels over eight hours. Ask questions as previously suggested. Then let them make up their own time graph within the same theme and make up their own questions to ask and answer.

In Year 5, the children need to recap and consolidate all the types of charts and graphs considered in previous years. They also need to investigate timetables.

Give children a timetable similar to this:

Station	Time				
Smithtown	06:35	07.15	08:30	10:10	12:50
Burntwood	07:25	08:00	09:25	11:10	13:55
Cheadle	08:35	09:05	10:35	12:25	14:50
Smallville	09:30	10:55	11:25	13:20	15:55
Edenford	10:15	11:40	12:15	14:25	17:05

From this purely fictional train timetable you can ask the children questions that involve finding sums and differences. For example,

■ Which is the shortest journey time from Smithtown to Burntwood?

■ How long does it take the 07:15 train from Smithtown to get to Edenford?

■ Sam has just missed the 09:05 train from Cheadle. How long does she have to wait until the next one?

■ Ben lives in Burntwood and wants to get to Smallville by 11:30. Which train should he catch? Why did you make that decision?

Encourage the children to use time number lines to help them count on and back.

Real bus, train and flight tables are good resources for this type of work, and they can be easily found on the internet.

In Year 6, children recap and consolidate all statistics worked on previously. One part of their new learning in this area is pie charts. Pies charts link well with fractions and percentages. You will find something written about this in the section on numerical reasoning.

Time

Finding time differences and durations is an obvious link to addition and subtraction. But first we need to consider the process of telling the time.

The national curriculum requires children in Year 2 to compare and sequence intervals of time, tell and write the time to five minutes, including quarter past/to the hour and draw the hands on a clock face to show these times. They also need to know the number of minutes in an hour and the number of hours in a day.

Digital time is not mentioned in Key Stage 1. Yet, digital time is probably the most common form of time that children see these days on phones, iPads, alarm clocks, the television and numerous other places.

In Year 3 the children are required to

■ tell and write the time from an analogue clock, including using Roman numerals from I to XII, and 12-hour and 24-hour clocks

■ estimate and read time with increasing accuracy to the nearest minute; record and compare time in terms of seconds, minutes and hours; use vocabulary such as o'clock, a.m./p.m., morning, afternoon, noon and midnight

■ know the number of seconds in a minute and the number of days in each month, year and leap year

■ durations of events [for example, to calculate the time taken by particular events or tasks].

The expectations for Year 3 children are massive! A lot of children struggle to tell the time in Key Stage 1 and Key Stage 2. I think there are various reasons for this, such as 'past' and 'to' times, which can be confusing, and having to ignore 'to' times when linking to digital time. Also, children are told what to do and when to do it. So, they do not actually need to know how to tell the time! We often tell a class, for example, that they have two minutes to clear away and five minutes later they are still clearing up. When it becomes important to them, they generally learn it then.

We recently gave three classes of Year 4 children a very short assessment on their understanding of time. They were given a clock face showing 20 minutes past two and asked to write this time in as many ways as they could. We also asked them to list the units used for time. More than 60% of children in the three classes could not answer. Really worrying!

We therefore need to ensure that we put into place a sensible progression for teaching time. We begin by teaching the children in Year 2 past times and link these to digital time. They count in 5s and can link the 5s to the hour numbers on the clock. The following number line is a helpful visual for this.

With practice, they can link, for example, 20 minutes past three and 3.20, 50 minutes past six and 6:50. Once the children are confident at telling past times and linking to digital, we ask them to investigate how many minutes until the next hour. We encourage them to count on in five-minute intervals. Our expectation for Year 2 is that they can tell time in three different ways, for example, 25 minutes past 4, 4:25 and 35 minutes to five, 50 minutes past 11, 11:50 and 10 minutes to 12.

Year 1 should learn about quarter past, half past and quarter to. A sensible link would be quarters and halves in fractions. The national curriculum expects children to tell o'clock and half-past time. However, if using number of the week in Year R, as described in the Number Sense section, these children will be able to tell o'clock time on analogue and digital clocks by the time they arrive in Year 1. Some can tell half-past times as well. So, as described, extending the requirements like this for children makes sense.

If children can confidently tell the time to five minutes on analogue and digital clocks by the end of Year 2, they are in a good position to make sufficient progress in Year 3, where they learn to read the time to the nearest minute on analogue, 12-hour and 24-hour clocks.

The following visual representation is helpful for introducing 24-hour time.

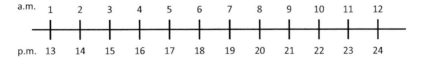

It is expected that children will have mastered time by the end of Year 4 and then use their understanding to solve problems, convert between units of time and read timetables. Therefore, teaching this right, so that Year 5 and 6 children can concentrate on what they are required to learn in their year groups is so important.

Using addition and subtraction to find differences and durations in time

Timelines are a great representation that we use to find time differences and durations. We should be asking children to solve problems that involve using these. The following are some examples of problems and suggestions on how to solve them.

> Frankie went to play football. He left home at 4:10 and arrived back after the match at 6:45. How long was he away from home?

For this problem, children need to count on from 4:10 to 6:45. They could do this by counting up to the next hour by adding 50 minutes. They could then add another hour and then 45 minutes to give a length of time of 2 hours 35 minutes.

> Ruby went swimming. She got into the pool at 3:55 and stayed in there for 90 minutes. What time did she get out?

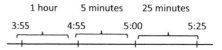

For this problem, children need to know that 90 minutes is equivalent to 1 hour 30 minutes. They can then add 1 hour. They would then partition 30 minutes into 5 minutes to make the next hour and 25 minutes.

> Freddie and Millie were doing their homework. They both started at 5:15. Freddie took 65 minutes. Millie took 16 minutes longer. At what time did Millie finish her homework?

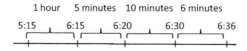

For this problem, children could add 1 hour first and then the extra 5 minutes. They could partition 16 into 10 to make 6:30 and 6 minutes.

> Jack and Olivia were going on holiday. Their flight was leaving at 7 a.m. They needed to be at the airport 90 minutes before take-off. Their journey to the airport will take 45 minutes. At what time do they need to leave home?

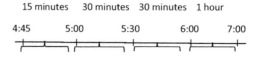

For this problem, children need to work back from seven o'clock. If Jack and Olivia need to be at the airport 90 minutes before 7:00, the children would partition 90 minutes into

1 hour and 30 minutes. They subtract 1 hour to make 6:00 and then 30 minutes to make 5:30. If the journey is 45 minutes, they would partition 45 minutes into 30 minutes and 15 minutes. They subtract 30 minutes to make 5:00 and then 15 minutes to make 4:45 which is the time Jack and Olivia need to leave home.

We should encourage children to partition times into useful chunks to help them solve time problems more easily and to become flexible thinkers.

Suggested progression for teaching addition and subtraction

This table sums up a suggested progression in addition and subtraction that we are working on in some schools. I hope that you will find this helpful.

Year R	Concentrate on adding and subtracting numbers to 10; create eight facts verbally and/or in writing to show commutativity, inverse and a different position for the equal to symbol, e.g., $4 + 3 = 7, 3 + 4 = 7, 7-4 = 3, 7-3 = 4, 7 = 3 + 4, 7 = 4 + 3, 3 = 7 - 4, 4 = 7 - 3$.
Year 1	Begin to develop mental calculation strategies, particularly those relating to knowing number pairs to 10, to add and subtract one-digit and two-digit numbers to 20 and then to 50, including within contexts of measurement; estimate and check answers using the inverse operation; solve problems involving addition and subtraction where children need to work out what to do.
Year 2	Continue to develop mental calculation strategies to add two-digit numbers and ones, two-digit numbers and 10s, two two-digit numbers and three one-digit numbers, including within the context of measurement; understand and carry out calculations that need exchange; estimate and check answers using the inverse operation; at end of Year 2, set addition calculations out vertically and use an expanded method; solve problems involving addition and subtraction where children need to work out what to do.
Year 3	Rehearse, consolidate and deepen mental calculation strategies to add and subtract appropriate numbers, including a three-digit number and ones, a three-digit number and 10s, a three-digit number and 100s; add and subtract numbers with up to three digits, using formal column written methods; add numbers with one decimal place within context of centimetres and millimetres; estimate and check answers using the inverse operation; solve problems involving addition and subtraction where children need to work out what to do.
Year 4	Rehearse, consolidate and deepen mental calculation strategies to add and subtract appropriate numbers, including up to four-digit numbers; add and subtract numbers, with up to four digits, using formal column written methods; add numbers with two decimal places within context of centimetres and millimetres and metres and centimetres; estimate and check answers using the inverse operation; solve problems involving addition and subtraction where children need to work out what to do

Year 5	Rehearse, consolidate and deepen mental calculation strategies to add and subtract appropriate numbers, including numbers greater than four digits; add and subtract numbers, with more than four digits, using formal column written methods; add numbers with three decimal places within context of distance, mass, volume and capacity; estimate and check answers using the inverse operation; solve problems involving addition and subtraction where children need to work out what to do
Year 6	Recap prior learning and continue to practice within the context of measures, estimating and checking answers, using mental calculation strategies as well as written methods and solving problems

References

Ching, BHH, *The importance of additive reasoning in children's mathematical achievement: A longitudinal study*, Oxford, Oxford University Press, 2017.

National Numeracy Strategy ITPs.

National Numeracy Strategy, Teaching mental calculation strategies guidance for teachers at key stages 1 and 2, https://www.stem.org.uk/elibrary/resource/29219, 1999.

4

Multiplicative reasoning

This section includes:

- Structures for multiplication
- Structures for division
- Relationships between multiplication and division
- Mental calculation strategies
- The progression through multiplication
- The progression through division
- Scaling up and the link to ratio
- Scaling down and the link to ratio
- Solving problems with multiplication and division
- Solving problems with all four operations
- Factors and multiples
- Order of operations
- Multiplying and links to perimeter
- Square numbers and links to area
- Cube numbers and links to volume
- Using statistics to practise multiplication and division
- Suggested progression for teaching multiplication and division

Introduction

Multiplicative reasoning

Multiplicative reasoning refers to the ability to solve problems arising from proportional situations. These situations often involve an understanding and application of, for example, multiplication and corresponding division facts, fractions, decimals, percentages and ratios.

Multiplicative reasoning often does not get much of a mention in primary mathematics. However, it is a very important concept and one we need to know about because a lot of what we need to teach in the national curriculum is based on the expectation that children can reason in a multiplicative way. It enables children to develop a deeper understanding of multiplicative structures such as fractions and ratio.

It has been suggested by research that many pupils (and adults) fail to move on from additive structures and this can lead to many misconceptions and errors in subsequent mathematical study.

(National Centre for Excellence in Teaching Mathematics [NCETM] July 2013; https://www.ncetm.org.uk/)

Many children will, for example, say that to make 2 into 10 you add 8 or to make 5 into 10 you add 5. This is additive thinking. If they were thinking multiplicatively, they would multiply 2 by 5 or 5 by 2 to make 10. Purely thinking in an additive way, as research suggests, can put a ceiling on children's learning. In the national curriculum, various topics need an understanding of multiplicative reasoning, for example, multiplication, division, scaling, area, volume, ratio and proportion. Teaching the children this concept is useful as it also helps build mental calculation strategies and develop reasoning. Multiplicative reasoning is essentially a recognition and use of grouping in the underlying pattern and structure of our number system.

Multiplicative reasoning contributes to an understanding of place value. The multiplicative aspect of place value tells us that we multiply the digit by the value of its position. The base 10 aspect tells us that our number system increases and decreases by powers of 10. To really understand these, the children need to have an understanding of multiplication.

Multiplicative reasoning makes it possible for children to see different kinds of relationships between numbers. When we ask children to count in steps of different sizes, we are helping them make the transition from additive to multiplicative reasoning because this shows the structure and efficiency of counting in groups and highlights sequences and patterns. When we do this with our children, modelling with manipulatives, such as towers of interlocking cubes, and visual representations, such as shapes on a whiteboard, is important so that these orders are learned with meaning and not simply as a rote counting method, which often happens and results in the children not truly understanding the patterns and sequences they are saying.

Structures for multiplication

There are two structures for multiplication. These are grouping and scaling.

Grouping is when we have a group of items, or a number, multiple times.

Diagram 4.1

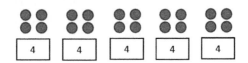

In this example, a unit of four presented five times. So, we have 4 multiplied by 5. Initially children are likely to count everything or add 4 five times. As they begin to recall multiplication facts, they will be able to multiply to give the product of 20.

The vocabulary used for multiplication is *multiplicand*, the number we start off with, *multiplied by the multiplier*, what we multiply by, *equals product*, the answer.

Multiplicand comes from the Latin word *multiplicandus*, which means 'to be multiplied'. *Multiplier* comes from the Latin word *multiplicāre*, which means 'to multiply'. *Product* comes from the Latin word *productum*, which means 'something produced'.

Different schools have different approaches to multiplication by grouping. Some talk in terms of 4 × 5 being four groups or lots of 5. Others talk of 4 × 5 as 4 multiplied by 5 or 5 groups or lots of 4. I advise teachers to teach the latter. One reason for this is that the multiplicand is the number we start with and the multiplier is what we do to it. This is consistent with the other three operations:

> 6 + 2; the augend is 6, and we add 2 onto it.
> 6 − 2; the minuend is 6, and we subtract 2 from it.
> 6 ÷ 2; 6 is the dividend is 6, and we make groups of two from it.

So, it makes sense to have 6 as the multiplicand and to multiply it by 2 or make two groups of 6.

When children are in Key Stage 2, they answer multiplication calculations, for example, 345 × 6. Children generally multiply 346 six times rather than talk about 346 groups or lots of 6.

The important message here is the school needs to decide which approach to take from the beginning of a child's journey through multiplication and follow it through. Mixing the two approaches causes confusion for some children, and these children will not develop a deep understanding of this operation.

Scaling, when used in multiplication, is when something, which could be a creature, object or number, is made greater by a specific amount. Demonstrating this through photographs or pictures of, for example, an enlarged ant or spider, is a good idea. Children are likely to be familiar with this from experiences outside school.

Diagram 4.2

In this example, 4 has been scaled up three times to give a product of 12.

Problem solving is where we usually scale; for example, 'Martha baked six cookies. Yasmine baked four times as many cookies. How many more cookies did Yasmine bake?'

Using counters to model problems such as the following is helpful:

Martha's cookies

Yasmine's cookies

If the counter representing Martha's biscuits is worth 6, then Yasmine baked 24 biscuits, 18 more than Martha.

Structures for division

There are three structures for division. These are grouping, scaling and sharing.

Grouping for division is the inverse of grouping for multiplication. So, instead of repeatedly adding groups, groups are subtracted, and we find out how many groups of a certain size we can make from the whole. Children will begin physically subtracting. As they begin to recall multiplication facts and their corresponding division facts, they move away from repeated subtraction and use these.

Diagram 4.3

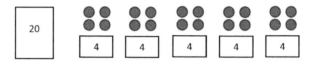

In this example, the whole is 20, and we can subtract five groups of 4.

The children would be asked grouping problems, such as

> The pet shop owner received a delivery of 20 goldfish. He put the goldfish into bowls. He put two goldfish into each bowl. How many bowls did he use?

In the Interactive Teaching Programme of the National Numeracy Strategy (NSS), grouping is helpful for demonstrating this concept.

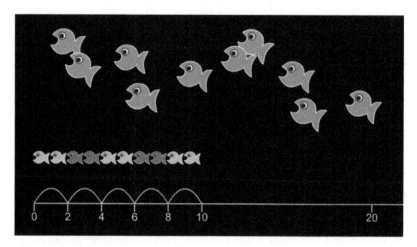

When clicking on two fish at a time, they are moved onto the number line. When all the fish have been moved, we can see that the pet-shop owner uses 10 bowls.

The vocabulary for division is *dividend*, the number we start with, divided by *divisor*, the size of the group we subtract, *equals quotient*, how many groups.

Dividend comes from the Latin word *dividendum*, which means 'portion or share'. *Divisor* comes from the Latin word *divisor* or 'divider', which is the number another number is divided by. *Quotient* comes from the Latin word *quotiens*, which means 'how many times'.

Scaling for division is the inverse of scaling for multiplication. Scaling for division links very well with fractions. In multiplication, we scale up; in division, we scale down. Scaling down means to make something smaller, for example, one third of the size, one eighth of the size. Showing photographs of the children is a great way to model this. The children can clearly see that their photograph is smaller than they actually are but that it is in proportion, so it has been scaled down.

In problem solving, we usually scaling; for example, 'Bertie had a dog which had a mass of 25 kg. Zac had a dog that was one fifth as heavy. How much heavier is Bertie's dog than Zac's?' Again, using counters to model the problem is helpful:

Bertie's dog
Zac's dog

If the counters for the mass of Bertie's dog represent 25 kg, each counter must be worth 5 kg. So, Zac's dog must be 5 kg, making Bertie's dog 20 kg heavier.

The third structure for division is sharing. This is not the inverse of multiplication. However, as with scaling, it links really well with fractions. Sharing is dividing an amount equally between a certain number of groups.

Children would be asked a problem, such as

Sophie had 45 marbles. She shared them equally into five bags. How many marbles are in each bag?

Some teachers encourage children to draw sharing circles. The bar model is possibly a better one to use. It is certainly tidier!

Diagram 4.4

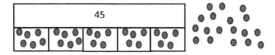

Children could share 45 counters or draw their own visual representation sharing into each of the five parts one at a time. They should be able to tell you that 45 marbles shared into 5 bags would give 9 marbles in each bag. So each bag holds one fifth of the marbles. Two fifths would be 18; three fifths, 27; and four fifths, 36.

Relationships between multiplication and division

As previously mentioned, multiplication and division are inverse operations. We can use multiplication to check a division by multiplying the quotient by the divisor to see if we get the dividend. We can use division to check a multiplication by dividing the product by the multiplier to see if we get the multiplicand. One requirement in the national curriculum is that children check answers to a calculation using the inverse operation. As mentioned in the Additive Reasoning section, I always give children calculators to check using the inverse because getting into the habit of checking is important, but we do not want to make it laborious for them by giving them too much to calculate, particularly if the operation is not one they are focusing on in the lesson.

Multiplication is commutative; division is not commutative. Both ideas need exploring with the children from the beginning. For example, $2 \times 4 = 4 \times 2$; $8 \div 4 = 2$, but $4 \div 8$ does not equal 2. Telling children that $4 \div 8$ cannot be done is incorrect. It can; the quotient is one half, or 0.5.

We also need to introduce the words *factor* and *multiple* when we are teaching both the concepts of multiplication and division. A multiplication calculation could be described as factor multiplied by factor equals multiple. A division calculation could be described as multiple divided by factor equals factor.

A multiple is a number that results when multiplying two numbers together. A factor is a number that makes a multiple. The children need to understand what these terms mean. There is more on factors and multiples later in this section.

Laws of multiplication

As well as being commutative, two other laws apply to multiplication. These are the associative law and the distributive law.

The associative law dictates that we can associate or combine the numbers in different orders. For example, if multiplying 25, 2 and 5, we could multiply 25 and 5 together first and then multiply by 2; we could multiply 2 and 25 together and then multiply by 5, or we could multiply 2 and 5 together and then multiply that by 25. All three ways will give a product of 250. Sharing this with the children so that they will be in a position to choose which way round they multiply three or more numbers is important.

This also applies to addition. For example, if adding 12, 25 and 18, we could use number pairs to 10 and add 12 and 18 together and then add the 25; we could add 12 and 25 together and then 18; or we could add 25 and 18 together and then 12. All three will give a sum or total of 55.

The distributive law is when one factor is distributed and separately applied to the other two parts. An example of this could be 14×12, which could become $(7 + 7) \times 12$, which then can be distributed to make $(7 \times 12) + (7 \times 12)$, which is $84 + 84$, giving a product of 168. Sharing this with the children is important because, if they can make sense of this, it will enable them to make multiplication calculations simpler. This fits well with the grid method for multiplication for example, 38×3 as shown in the following.

Diagram 4.5

	30	8
3	90	24

In this example, we have made the calculation $(30 \times 3) + (8 \times 3)$, giving a product of 114.

Mental calculation strategies

As with addition and subtraction, we need to teach mental calculation strategies for multiplication and division. The NSS encouraged teachers to teach the following:

- Multiplication and division facts
- Partitioning
- Multiplying by 4 by doubling and doubling again
- Multiplying by 5 by multiplying by 10 and halving
- Multiplying by 20 by multiplying by 10 and doubling
- Multiplying by 15 by multiplying by 10, halving for multiplying by 5 and adding the two together
- Dividing 4 by halving and halving again
- Dividing by 5 by dividing by 10 and doubling
- Dividing by 20 by dividing by 10 and halving
- Using the relationship between the four operations
- Using known facts

This means that we need to be very careful what multipliers and divisors to put in a calculation when we want the children to learn about written methods. Good multipliers and divisors for mental calculation strategies are 2, 4, 5 and 10. 3, 6, 7, 8 and 9 make good multipliers and divisors when teaching written methods.

As mentioned in additive reasoning, we want children to be flexible thinkers, so we do need to devote some time to teach and for children to practise and consolidate these strategies. The planning used in some schools devotes two or three weeks to this before teaching written methods.

Multiplication and division facts

The children need to start learning multiplication facts and corresponding division facts up to 12 multiplied by 12. They begin this in Early Years Foundation Stage (EYFS), when they count in steps of 1 and 10 and possibly 5 and 2. I advise EYFS teachers to ask the children to put up their fingers as they count in these steps and ask how many lots of, for example, one when they have their fifth finger and to say that this is 1 multiplied by 5 which equals 5. If children are counting in 10s, again, they use their fingers, and the teacher could stop when the seventh finger is showing, ask how many lots of 10 and say, 'This is 10 multiplied by 7, which equals 70.' This process familiarises children with the pattern of the multiplication tables. In Year 4, children are tested on their recall of the multiplication facts, so we need to start counting in steps and making the link to these facts early in a child's education. Obviously, we would not expect children to have a quick recall of multiplication tables for 1, 10, 5 and 2 in EYFS, just a familiarisation with them that can be built on in subsequent years.

If children understand the commutativity of multiplication, we can help them to understand that they only need to know half of the 144 facts. If they know the $9 \times 7 = 63$, they also know that $7 \times 9 = 63$ so that instantly reduces the facts they need to know to 72! We also need to build in the corresponding division facts. If they know $9 \times 7 = 63$, they also know that $63 \div 7 = 9$ and $63 \div 9 = 7$.

Some years ago, I saw a multiplication fact chart that was used in Shanghai. It was so sensible that I copied the idea and made my own. In this country, we do not usually include the facts for one. This is important as it sets the basis of the pattern of multiplication facts children need to learn.

$1 \times 1 = 1$	$2 \times 2 = 4$	$3 \times 3 = 9$	$4 \times 4 = 16$	$5 \times 5 = 25$	$6 \times 6 = 36$	$7 \times 7 = 49$	$8 \times 8 = 64$
$2 \times 1 = 2$	$3 \times 2 = 6$	$4 \times 3 = 12$	$5 \times 4 = 20$	$6 \times 5 = 30$	$7 \times 6 = 42$	$8 \times 7 = 56$	$9 \times 8 = 72$
$3 \times 1 = 3$	$4 \times 2 = 8$	$5 \times 3 = 15$	$6 \times 4 = 24$	$7 \times 5 = 35$	$8 \times 6 = 48$	$9 \times 7 = 63$	$10 \times 8 = 80$
$4 \times 1 = 4$	$5 \times 2 = 10$	$6 \times 3 = 18$	$7 \times 4 = 28$	$8 \times 5 = 40$	$9 \times 6 = 54$	$10 \times 7 = 70$	$11 \times 8 = 88$
$5 \times 1 = 5$	$6 \times 2 = 12$	$7 \times 3 = 21$	$8 \times 4 = 32$	$9 \times 5 = 45$	$10 \times 6 = 60$	$11 \times 7 = 77$	$12 \times 8 = 96$
$6 \times 1 = 6$	$7 \times 2 = 14$	$8 \times 3 = 24$	$9 \times 4 = 36$	$10 \times 5 = 50$	$11 \times 6 = 66$	$12 \times 7 = 84$	
$7 \times 1 = 7$	$8 \times 2 = 16$	$9 \times 3 = 27$	$10 \times 4 = 40$	$11 \times 5 = 55$	$12 \times 6 = 72$		
$8 \times 1 = 8$	$9 \times 2 = 18$	$10 \times 3 = 30$	$11 \times 4 = 44$	$12 \times 5 = 60$			
$9 \times 1 = 9$	$10 \times 2 = 20$	$11 \times 3 = 33$	$12 \times 4 = 48$				
$10 \times 1 = 10$	$11 \times 2 = 22$	$12 \times 3 = 36$					
$11 \times 1 = 11$	$12 \times 2 = 24$						
$12 \times 1 = 12$							

$9 \times 9 = 81$	$10 \times 10 = 100$	$11 \times 11 = 121$	$12 \times 12 = 144$
$10 \times 9 = 90$	$11 \times 10 = 110$	$12 \times 11 = 132$	
$11 \times 9 = 99$	$12 \times 10 = 120$		
$12 \times 9 = 108$			

This chart highlights the commutativity of multiplication. It also shows that, if rapid recall is not something that some children can achieve, there are other ways to work out the facts; for example, if children cannot remember the multiplication facts for 7, they can multiply by 5 and 2 and add the two products together. This is shown by the arrangement of the shapes.

This progression in teaching these facts might be worth considering: counting in steps of 1, 10 and 5 in EYFS as described earlier, learning these facts in Year 1, consolidating these facts in Year 2 and beginning to learn those for 2, 4 and 3. The reason for suggesting these is that the facts for 4 and double those for 2 and the facts for 3 will be helpful for when children find thirds in fractions. In Year 3, children consolidate the multiplication and division facts for 1, 10, 5, 2, 4 and 3 and then work on facts for 8, which are double the facts for 4; 6, which are double the facts for 3; and 12, which are double the facts for 6. In Year 4, they consolidate all learned so far and then work on the facts for 7, 9 and 11. If taking commutativity into consideration, there will only be a few new facts to learn: $7 \times 7 = 49, 9 \times 7 = 63, 11 \times 7 = 77, 9 \times 9 = 81, 11 \times 9 = 99$ and $11 \times 11 = 121$.

Looking at the patterns that these facts make is helpful. For example, with the multiplication facts for 9, the 10s number increases by one, and the 1s number decreases by one, making a pattern of 9, 18, 27, 36, 45, 54, 63, 72, 81, 90, 108. Noting that the numbers alternate odd, even, odd, even and that the digit total is always 9 is also interesting. The digit total is found by adding the digits which make up the product; for example, $2 + 7 = 9$.

You can also see that the digits are reversed as the facts increase, for example, 18, 81, 27, 72, 36 and 63.

With the facts for 3, the order is odd, even, odd, even, and the digit total adds up to 3, 6 and 9. The facts for 6 are all even, and their digit totals also add up to 3, 6 and 9. If we know digit totals we can work out which numbers are multiples of 3, 6 and 9 and divisible by these divisors.

The digit total for 369 is 9 ($3 + 6 + 9 = 18, 1 + 8 = 9$). We therefore know that it is a multiple of and divisible by three and nine. It is not a multiple of six because it an odd number. The digit total for 684 is 9. It is even, so 684 is a multiple of 3, 6 and 9 and divisible by these numbers.

The facts for 12 are all even, and their digit totals again add up to 3, 6 and 9. The divisibility rule for 12 is that it needs to be both divisible by 3 and 4.

The facts for 2, 4 and 8, are all even. A multiple of two ends with 2, 4, 6, 8 or 0. We also know that numbers ending with these digits are divisible by 2. We know a number is a multiple of and divisible by 4 if the last two digits are a multiple of 4. For example, 624 is both a multiple of 4 and divisible by 4 because the last part of the number is 24, which is a multiple of 4. We know a number is a multiple of and divisible by 8 if the last three digits are a multiple of 8. For example, 3104 is a multiple of and divisible by 8 because 104 is a multiple of 8.

Obviously, a multiple of 10 must end with zero, and multiples of 5 alternate with a 5 and a zero.

We need to give the children the opportunity to explore these.

Partitioning

When children multiply and divide, they need to look at numbers and see if they can answer them efficiently using a mental calculation and not always default to the written method. For example, 56×3, can be answered using a partitioning method. Children could partition 56 into 50 and 6 and multiply 50 by 3 using their multiplication facts: $5 \times 3 = 15$, so 50×3 must be 150. The product must be 168 because 6×3 is 18 and $150 + 18 = 168$. Of course, children can make jottings; the expectation is not that they hold the parts in their heads.

For 175×3, we can use the following model, this time partitioning into 150 and 25. If they know $15 \times 3 = 45$, they should be able to tell you that $150 \times 3 = 450$. They can then double 25 and add another to give 75. They combine the two parts to give a product of 525.

Diagram 4.6

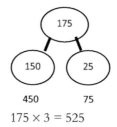

450　　　75

$175 \times 3 = 525$

For division, it is helpful to begin to teach this strategy by exploring ways to partition numbers into multiples of ten and whatever is left. For example, 72 can be partitioned into 70 and 2, 60 and 12, 50 and 22, 40 and 32, 30 and 42, 20 and 52 and 10 and 62. If children are fluent in partitioning in this way in Year 3 and need, for example, to divide 72 by 2, they can partition 72 into 60 and 12. They can use their multiplication facts to work out that $60 \div 2 = 30$ ($2 \times 3 = 6$, so $20 \times 3 = 60$) and $12 \div 3 = 4$, so the quotient must be 20 add 4, which is 24.

Diagram 4.7

This model is a helpful one to use:

$45 \div 3$

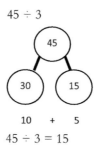

10　　+　　5

$45 \div 3 = 15$

Children partition 45 into 30 and 15. They know that 30 is the 10th multiple of 3 and that 15 is the 5th multiple of 3. So, they write 10 and 5 and combine them to make 15, which is the quotient for $45 \div 3$.

In Year 4, they would find different ways to partition three-digit numbers into a multiple of 10 and the rest of the number. For example, 164 can be partitioned into 160 and 4, 150 and 14, 140 and 24, 130 and 34 and so on. They could then divide 164 by 3 by partitioning 164 into 150 and 14 and divide as described for Year 3.

Diagram 4.8

Again, this model is helpful:

$135 \div 3$

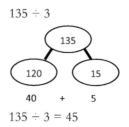

40　　+　　5

$135 \div 3 = 45$

We partition into 120 because the children know that $4 \times 3 = 12$, so $12 \div 3$ is 4, so $120 \div 3$ must be 40. They can then use their multiplication and division facts to work out $15 \div 3$ is 5.

Multiplying by 4 by doubling and doubling again

Children have been doubling since Year R; however, little reference to doubling and halving is made in the national curriculum. They are useful tools for mental calculation, so we need to keep using them. If children are multiplying by 4, they should use a doubling-and-doubling-again strategy, maybe not for a large number when a written method might be more efficient. However, a good expectation could be that they use this strategy as a way of checking.

Here are some examples:

$$48 \times 4$$

Children could partition 48 into 40 and 8, double each number twice to make 160 and 32 and recombine them to give a product of 192. They should be encouraged to use jottings.

$$296 \times 4$$

Children could partition 296 into 200 and 90 and 6, double each number twice to make 800, 360 and 24 and recombine them to give a product of 1184.

Multiplying by 5 by multiplying by 10 and halving

Children should know the relationship between 5 and 10: that 5 is half of 10 and that 10 is double 5. When they know this, they should explore this strategy for multiplication.

For example, for 72 multiplied by 5, the children multiply by 10 to give 720 and then halve it to give 360.

$$463 \times 5$$

The children multiply by 10 to give 4630 and then halve it to give a product of 2315.

Of course, they could halve the multiplicand first and then multiply by 10.

Again, they use jottings to keep track of what they are doing.

Multiplying by 20 by multiplying by 10 and doubling

Children should know that 20 is double 10, so they can use this to multiply, for example, 284 by 20 by multiplying by 10 to give 2840 and then doubling to give a product of 5680. Alternatively, they could double the multiplicand first and then multiply by 10.

$$84 \times 20$$

This could be solved by doubling 84, double 80 is 160 and double 4 is 8, recombining to make 168 and then multiply by 10 to give a product of 1680.

Multiplying by 15 by multiplying by 10, halving for multiplying by 5 and adding the two together

This is a sensible strategy to use for multiplying by 15.

Here are some examples:

$$48 \times 15$$

The children multiply by 10 to give 480. They then halve this, so gives 240. They then add the two the numbers to give a product of 720.

$$536 \times 15$$

Multiply 536 by 10 to give 5360; halve it, maybe by partitioning into 5000, 300 and 60, to give 2500, 150 and 30; then recombine to give 2680. Finally, add 5360 and 2680 to give a product of 8040.

Dividing by 4 by halving and halving again

This strategy is the inverse of the one suggested for multiplying by four.

For example,

$$86 \div 4$$

Half of 86 is 43. Half of 43 is 21.5. Numbers that give a quotient with one decimal place could be given to Year 3 because of their work in place value.

$$125 \div 4$$

Half of 120 is 60. Half of 60 is 30. Half of 5 is 2.5. Half of 2.5 is 1.25. So, the quotient is 31.25. These could be given to Year 4 children to explore because of their work on hundredths in place value.

Dividing by 5 by dividing by 10 and doubling

If we multiplied by 10 and halve for multiplying by 5, we should have a pretty good idea that when dividing by 5, we would do the inverse: divide by 10 and double. We double because we are subtracting groups of 5, which is less than groups of 10.

For example,

$$240 \div 5$$

First, we divide by 10 to give 24. We only need groups of 5, not 10, so we double to give a quotient of 48:

$$458 \div 5$$

First, divide by 10 to give 45.8. We only groups of 5, not 10, so we double to give a quotient of 91.6.

Dividing by 20 by dividing by 10 and halving

If we multiplied by 10 and double for multiplying by 20, we need to do the inverse for dividing by 20, divide by 10 and halve.

For example,

$$360 \div 20$$

First, we divide by 10 to give 36. We need 20 groups, not 10, so we halve it to give a quotient of 18.

$$1356 \div 20$$

First, divide by 10 to give 135.6. We need groups of 20, not 10, so we halve it to give a quotient of 67.8.

Using patterns of similar calculations

As mentioned in additive reasoning, this is similar to variation. If the children know that $6 \times 3 = 18$, they should be able to tell you other facts; for example,

- $7 \times 3 = 21$; because there is one more group of 3, 3 needs to be added on to 18.
- $6 \times 4 = 24$; because there is one more group of 6, the answer must be 6 more than 18.

They should be able to make up a lot of other facts without calculating because of what they notice and the patterns they see. We do not give the children enough opportunities to think like this, so they tend to calculate everything when they could just look for patterns.

Use relationships between operations

Understanding commutativity and inverse are really important. If the children really understand these concepts, they will be able to use them to make simple mental calculations. For example, if they know that 6 multiplied by 2 equals 12, they should be able to use that to work out the product of 12 divided by 2.

Children seeing the links between multiplication and repeated addition, for example, $6 \times 2 = 6 + 6 = 2 + 2 + 2 + 2 + 2 + 2 = 12$, is important. This will help them in Year 5 when they need to learn how to multiply fractions by whole numbers, for example, three fifths multiplied by 3 is three fifths add three fifths add three fifths, which is nine fifths or one whole and four fifths.

They need to link division with repeated subtraction, for example, $12 \div 6$, which means we can subtract two groups of 6 from 12. Sometimes these relationships get lost towards the end of Key Stage 2 when children tend to default to written methods for the four operations.

Using known number facts

Using known number facts to derive others is a great way to help children become flexible thinkers. Writing a fact on the board and asking children to write down as many other facts as they can in about three minutes is a good idea. Encouraging them to add, subtract, double and halve, multiply and divide by powers of 10 enables children to think and reason.

For example,

If I know that $7 \times 9 = 63$, I also know that . . .

- $7 \times 90 = 630$ (90 is 10 times greater than 9, so the product must be 10 times greater than 63)
- $14 \times 90 = 1260$ (7 has been doubled, so the earlier product of 630 must be doubled)
- $9 \times 7 = 63$ (commutativity)
- $63 \div 9 = 7$ (inverse operation)
- $14 \times 18 = 252$ (both 7 and 9 are doubled, so the product must be doubled twice)
- $7 \times 0.9 = 6.3$ (9 has been made 10 times smaller, so the product must be 10 times smaller)
- $3.5 \times 0.9 = 3.15$ (7 has been halved, so the earlier product of 6.3 must be halved)

The 2018 Standard Assessment Test Paper for arithmetic in Year 6 had a few questions which could have been answered quickly and efficiently using mental calculation strategies; for example,

$$2 \times 45 =$$

For this calculation, the children should have doubled 45.

$$838 \div 1 =$$

By Year 6, children should know that when they multiply or divide by one, the multiplicand or dividend remains unchanged.

$$99 \div 11 =$$

Children should know the multiplication and corresponding division facts for 11.

$$5 \times 4 \times 10 =$$

The children could have used the associative law and multiplied one pair of numbers together and then multiplied the product by the third number; for example, $5 \times 4 = 20$, and $20 \times 10 = 200$.

$$270 \div 3 =$$

Children should have used their multiplication and division facts; knowing $9 \times 3 = 27$ means they should know that $27 \div 3 = 9$, so $270 \div 3$ must be 90.

$$5\,400 \div 9 =$$

Again, multiplication and division facts; knowing $6 \times 9 = 54$ means they should know $54 \div 9 = 6$, so $5400 \div 9$ must be 600.

$$60 \div 15 =$$

Children could have used doubling 15 to 30, then again to give 60 to give a quotient of 4.

$$0.5 \times 28 =$$

If children make the link that 0.5 is half, they could just half 28 to give a product of 14, which, in effect, is the same as the strategy when we multiply by 10 and halve, only this time we adapt it to multiply by 1 and halve.

$$3.9 \times 30 =$$

The children could partition this into 3 and 0.9 and multiply each part by 3 and then 10: $3 \times 3 = 9$, so 3×30 must be 90; $0.9 \times 3 = 2.7$, so 0.9×30 must be 27; $90 + 27$ is equivalent to 117.

$$1\frac{1}{2} \times 40 =$$

If children have been carrying out activities as described in the part about using what you know, they might see that if we double one and a half and halve 40, we would have an equivalent calculation of 3×20, which gives a product of 60.

The squares on the assessment papers lead children towards a tendency to use written methods. They certainly do not encourage children to make jottings. We need to give them practice at doing this. Giving them plain paper to do this often helps.

The main message in this section of the book is that children should use mental calculation strategies, not standard written methods, as often as possible for the four operations unless a mental calculation strategy cannot be easily used or a written method would be more efficient or quicker.

The progression through multiplication

When beginning to teach the written method for multiplication to the children, we should begin by showing a series of calculations and discuss which methods would be best to use. By this time, they will have spent a few weeks revisiting and developing mental calculation strategies learned in previous years so will be in a position to make sensible decisions.

For example,

- 243 × 5 (multiplying by 10 and halving)
- 125 × 3 (partitioning into 120 and 5, multiplying by 3 and recombining)
- 225 × 15 (multiplying by 10, halving and adding the two products)
- 450 × 4 (doubling and doubling again)
- 350 × 20 (multiplying by 10 and doubling)
- 3537 × 7 (the written method because several exchanges are needed)

When teaching the written method for multiplication, introducing it when an exchange is needed is important. Calculations with no exchanges should be carried out using a mental calculation strategy; for example, 123 × 3 can be answered through partitioning. As mentioned in additive reasoning, if we start teaching the written method in Year 3 when it is not necessary, this gives the message that a written method is the one we need to use from now.

Of course, all the way through their learning of multiplication, children need to estimate the product and check using division with a calculator. They should also become increasingly familiar with the vocabulary of *multiplicand, multiplied by multiplier* and *equals product.*

Using manipulatives is vital to ensure that a child really understands what they are doing when they calculate.

In Year 1, the national curriculum expects children to solve one-step problems involving multiplication and division by calculating the answer using concrete objects, pictorial representations and arrays with the support of the teacher.

It is a good idea to begin by showing children a collection of real objects that show arrays, for example, even Numicon plates, egg boxes, bun tins or tins of food set out in an array, is a good idea. Ask children to talk about what they notice. Can they see, for example, two rows of six holes in the egg box and six rows of two? Can they tell you that there are 12 holes altogether? Can they see this as 6 + 6, 2 + 2 + 2 + 2 + 2 + 2, as six 2s and as two 6s to give a product of 12?

After they have explored the real arrays, let them draw pictures in their own way and write what they see in simple terms.

This could be repeated with pictures of arrays such as those that can be found on wallpaper or wrapping paper.

After exploring physically and visually, giving the children paper arrays such as the following makes sense:

Diagram 4.9

You could ask them to tell you the addition statement they can make (5 + 5 + 5 = 15) and then ask them to turn the array around and to tell you the new addition statement (3 + 3 + 3 + 3 + 3 = 15). Tell them that there is another way to record this. There are three groups of 5 or five groups of 3. Show them the multiplication statements 5 × 3 = 15, which means three groups of 5 or 5 multiplied by 3, and 3 × 5 = 15, which means five groups of 3 or 3 multiplied by 5. Using the words *multiplied by* right from the beginning is important because this indicates the operation. Remind children of commutativity for addition and let them know that multiplication is the same. Which way we multiply does not matter; the product is the same. Say statements together as a class; for example, 5 multiplied by 3 equals 15 and 3 multiplied by 5 equals 15 because multiplication is commutative.

Resources such as Numicon are helpful for reinforcing this concept.

Diagram 4.10

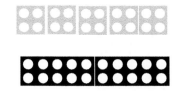

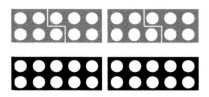

This shows that 4 multiplied by 5 is 20.

This shows the commutative fact that 5 multiplied by 4 is 20.

In Year 2, the national curriculum requires children to spend time exploring arrays. It is expected that children can recall and use multiplication and division facts for 2, 5 and 10. They are required to calculate mathematical statements for multiplication within the facts they are learning. It is expected that they understand commutativity. They should also be able to solve problems.

Children could begin by exploring what happens when multiplying by zero and 1. If there is nothing and we have nothing twice, we still have nothing. They need to understand that whatever we multiply zero by we will always have a product of zero. We can then use the commutative law and show the children that if we have a number and multiply that by zero, this would still give a product of zero. When multiplying a number by 1, the multiplicand will also be the product. If they have learned their multiplication facts for 1, they should be able to apply that to any number.

After multiplying by zero and 1, children could then explore what happens when multiplying by 10. We could begin by counting in 10s from zero to 120 and back again. A counting stick or something similar is useful. Children could count in multiples of 10 and you could stop at various positions, expecting the children to say how many lots of 10 make that number.

We could then give pairs of children 10 cubes. Ask them to put them in a line. What do they notice? Discuss the idea that they have one cube 10 times or 10 lots of one cube. We could then show them how this can be written as a calculation: $1 \times 10 = 10$. They could put the cubes together to make a tower. What do they notice this time? They should be able to say that there is one lot of 10 and show the calculation: $10 \times 1 = 10$. This is a different calculation, but it has the same product. We should reinforce the idea of commutativity for multiplication. Ask the children to put 20 cubes in a line in pairs. What do they think the calculation would be this time? They should be able to tell you it is $2 \times 10 = 20$. They make two towers of 10, which would be written as $10 \times 2 = 20$.

For higher numbers, arrays could be provided. The following is an example.

Diagram 4.11

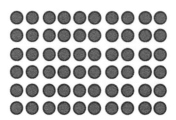

This array shows $10 \times 6 = 60$ and, looking at it the other way round, $6 \times 10 = 60$. Bringing out the idea that children can also say 10 sixes and 6 tens is helpful. At the same time, talking about taking groups of 10 and 6 away and helping them see that $60 \div 10 = 6$ and $60 \div 6 = 10$ are important. Repeating this with other examples for multiplication and division facts for 10 will help children understand the relationship between the two operations. Children should be asked to draw their own models and write the multiplication and division statements. Arrays are used to simply represent what they were doing with cubes in previous lessons.

We could then repeat this process for multiplying by 5 and 2.

After exploring multiplying by two, it is a good idea to explore even and then odd numbers. The national curriculum requires children to recognise odd and even numbers. This is the only time that they are specifically mentioned. However, we look at these when investigating numbers to 10 in Year R, so children may be familiar with them.

You could begin by asking them what they know about even numbers. Together count in multiples of 2 from zero to 24. Spend a short while talking about multiples. Let the children know that a multiple is the product of multiplying two numbers together. Go through a few of the multiplication facts for 10, 5 and 2, for example, $2 \times 10 = 20$,

$3 \times 5 = 15$ and $4 \times 2 = 8$, and highlight that the products of these are multiples of the multiplicand and multiplier.

Children need to know that multiples of 2 are always even numbers. Numicon plates are a good resource to demonstrate this. Even plates show that the numbers increase in pairs and that there is never one left over. All other numbers are odd and have an extra one. Odd Numicon plates demonstrate this well; children can clearly see the pairs and the extra one.

We need to make sure that children understand that zero means there is no amount. Very importantly, it also has the role of the placeholder and shows when there is no digit positioned in a particular position. When it is a placeholder in the ones position the number is a multiple of 2 and so is even. We can therefore say that zero is even.

Children should know that all numbers ending with 0, 2, 4, 6 and 8 are even and all numbers ending with 1, 3, 5, 7 and 9 are odd.

Allowing some time for the children to explore the result of adding, subtracting and multiplying pairs of even and odd numbers using Numicon is helpful. They should be able to tell you that adding, subtracting and multiplying pairs of even numbers always results in an even number, adding and subtracting pairs of odd numbers also results in an even sum or total and difference and multiplying odd numbers results in an odd product. It is worth exploring this further in Key Stage 2 and asking the children to make generalisations and prove that they are correct. See the appropriate section in the Numerical Reasoning section for ideas on this concept.

The array is an important visual for multiplication and division. Showing children real-life examples of arrays or photos of them, for example, egg boxes, bun trays, tiles and cars in a car park, is important.

Diagram 4.12

You could draw the following on the board.

Ask the children if this is an array. They should be able to tell you that it is not because an array is a pattern with equal rows and columns. You could invite someone to turn what you have done into an array.

The children could use counters to make this array. Drawing out the ideas of repeated addition $5 + 5 + 5$ and $3 + 3 + 3 + 3 + 3$ and grouping three groups of 5 and five groups of 3, if looking the other way around is important. How many are there altogether? When children are confident with arrays for multiplication, you could use the same arrays to focus on division and make the link to repeated subtraction.

Introducing the word *product* as the answer to a multiplication and *quotient* as the answer to a division is important, as is reinforcing commutativity and demonstrating that division is not commutative.

It is worth spending some time exploring various arrays focusing on a multiplier of three, these arrays could be made of coins or 1 cm cubes to bring in links to money and length. We should also be sure to ask problems; for example, 'Rachel had some pound coins; she made an array with them. There were 24 coins altogether. She made three rows of coins. How many coins were in each row?'

In Year 3, the requirements of the national curriculum are that children multiply and divide two-digit numbers by a single digit and use mental strategies, gradually moving towards the formal written method.

I always begin a series of lessons by exploring multiplication facts. We look at the 2s and 4s and then add the 8s, aiming for children to see that the facts for 4 are double those for 2 and that the facts for 8 are double those for 4. Cuisenaire rods is a good resource for this.

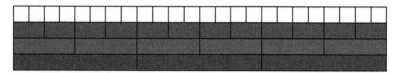

This black and white image of Cuisenaire shows that eight white squares, four red oblongs and two purple ones are equivalent to one brown oblong. We could say from this that 1 × 8 = 8, 2 × 4 = 8, 4 × 2 = 8 and 8 × 1 = 8. We can see that to multiply by 2 we double the facts for 1; to multiply by 4, we double the facts for 2; and to multiply by 8, we double the facts for 4. It is important that children see the relationship between these multiples. We could carry out similar activities for 3, 6 and 12.

Exploring patterns for 7, 9 and 11 are also interesting. Exploring different ways to find the products is helpful. For 7, we could do these $(6 \times 7) + (1 \times 7)$, $(5 \times 7) + (2 \times 7)$, $(4 \times 7) + (3 \times 7)$ or the other way around.

The facts for 11 show an interesting pattern: the digits are repeated for the facts to 9×11. Then, this happens:

$$10 \times 11 = 110$$
$$11 \times 11 = 121$$
$$12 \times 11 = 132$$
$$21 \times 11 = 231$$
$$25 \times 11 = 275$$
$$31 \times 11 = 341$$
$$42 \times 11 = 462$$

It is interesting to see what the children notice: for 10×11, add the two digits in the multiplicand and put the total between the two digits of the multiplier; for example, 1 add

0 equals 1; position the 1 between the 1 and the 0 to give 110. For 25 × 11, add 2 and 5 and then position the 7 between the 2 and the 5 to give the product of 275.

The national curriculum requires Year 3 to work towards the written method. It is expected that in Year 4 children have mastered this method for multiplying two- and three-digit numbers by a single digit.

Moving toward the written method for multiplication involves arrays and the grid model. The following is a good progression which makes a lot of sense.

The children can explore this using dotty paper, Dienes equipment and place-value counters.

Diagram 4.13

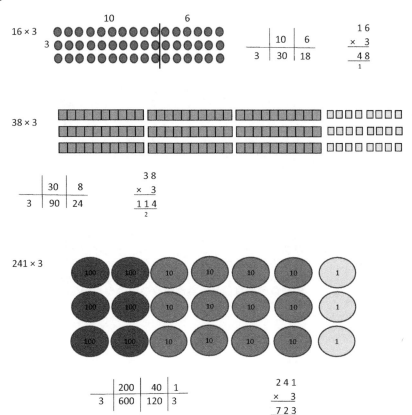

In Year 5, the children are expected to multiply up to four-digit numbers by a single digit. This is simply an extension of what they have done in previous years. Their new learning is long multiplication.

In the appendices of the national curriculum are these two examples of how this process could be carried out.

24 × 16 becomes	124 × 26 becomes	124 × 26 becomes
2	1 2	1 2
2 4	**1 2 4**	**1 2 4**
× **1 6**	× **2 6**	× **2 6**
2 4 0	**2 4 8 0**	**7 4 4**
1 4 4	**7 4 4**	**2 4 8 0**
3 8 4	**3 2 2 4**	**3 2 2 4**
	1 1	1 1
Answer: 384	Answer: 3224	Answer: 3224

Beginning this process by using arrays and the grid model similar to the ones that follow is helpful.

Diagram 4.14

24 × 16

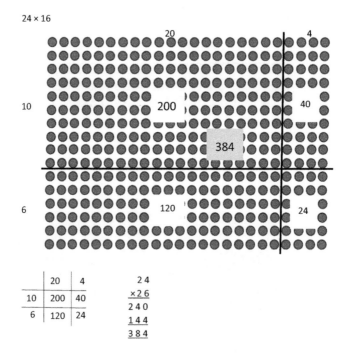

	20	4
10	200	40
6	120	24

```
  2 4
 ×2 6
 2 4 0
 1 4 4
 3 8 4
```

Some children may need time working on two separate calculations and then finding the sum or total, for example, 24 × 10 = 240 and 24 × 6 = 144, so 240 + 144 = 384, before they can confidently put them together for long multiplication.

It is expected that this concept is mastered in Year 5 so that when children move into Year 6, they solve problems involving a mixture of all four operations.

The progression through division

As for multiplication, when beginning to teach the written method for division to the children, we should begin by showing a series of calculations and discuss which methods would be best to use. By this time, they will have spent a few weeks revisiting and developing mental calculation strategies learned in previous years so will be in a position to make sensible decisions.

For example,

- 243 ÷ 5 (dividing by 10 and doubling)
- 72 ÷ 3 (partitioning into 60 and 12, divide and recombine)
- 225 ÷ 10 (using understanding of the base 10 element of place value)
- 480 ÷ 4 (halving and halving again)
- 260 ÷ 20 (dividing by 10 and halving)
- 1557 ÷ 7 (the written method because several exchanges are needed)

When teaching the written method for division, introducing it when an exchange is needed is important. Calculations with no exchange should be carried out using a mental calculation strategy; for example, 123 ÷ 3 can be answered through partitioning. If we start teaching the written method in Year 3 when it is not necessary, children usually use it as their default method.

Of course, all the way through their learning of division, children need to estimate the quotient and check it using multiplication with a calculator. They should also become increasingly familiar with the vocabulary of *dividend*, *divided by divisor* and *equals quotient*.

In Year 1, beginning division by showing children the same collection of real objects that show arrays that are the same as they used for multiplication, for example, even Numicon plates, egg boxes, bun tins or tins of food set out in an array, is a good idea. Ask children to talk about what they notice. Can they see, for example, two rows of six holes in the egg box and six rows of two? Can they tell you that there are 12 holes made up of two groups of 6 or six groups of 2? Can they see this as repeated subtraction, 12 subtract 6 and subtract another 6 and as 12 subtract 2 – 2 – 2 – 2 – 2 – 2?

After they have explored the real arrays, give them pictures and then let them draw similar pictures in their own way and write what they see in simple terms.

After exploring physically and visually, give the children the same paper arrays that they used for multiplication.

Diagram 4.15

Begin by recapping multiplication, including using repeated addition, the groups of approach and commutativity, and then discuss that the dividend is 15 and that we can make three groups of 5 or five groups of 3. We should link this to repeated subtraction. It is important that children develop an understanding of the relationship between the two operations.

Resources such as Numicon are helpful for reinforcing this.

Diagram 4.16

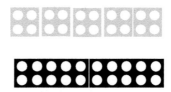

This shows that 4 multiplied by 5 is 20. It also shows that we can subtract 5 groups of 4 to give a quotient of 5.

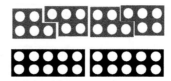

This shows the commutative fact that 5 multiplied by 4 is 20. It also shows that we can subtract 4 groups of 5 from 20 to give a quotient of 4.

In Year 2, children could begin by exploring what happens when they divide by 1. When dividing a number by 1, the dividend will also be the quotient. If they have learned their multiplication facts for 1, they should be able to apply that to dividing any number by 1.

After dividing by 1, the children could then explore what happens when dividing multiples of 10 by 10. Using place-value charts is a good idea. Children need to understand that when dividing by 10, a number is made 10 times smaller. For example, 70 divided by 10 is 7.

Giving children arrays, as for multiplication, to explore division is helpful.

Diagram 4.17

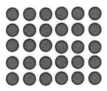

This array shows five rows of 6, or 6 + 6 + 6 + 6 + 6, which is 30. It also shows that we can take away groups of 6 from 30 and will end up with five groups of 6. If we look at the array the other way around, we can see that we can take away six groups of 5.

The array is perfect for showing commutativity and inverse and therefore the relationship between the two operations. These should always be included in any work on multiplying and dividing.

In Year 3, the national curriculum requires the children to write and calculate mathematical statements for division using the multiplication tables that they know, including two-digit numbers divided by one-digit numbers, using mental calculation and progressing to formal written methods.

We must not lose sight of the fact that the curriculum requires that children use the multiplication facts they know. This fits well with division using the mental calculation strategy of partitioning as described earlier in this section. In Years 4, 5 and 6, the require-ments continue to expect children to use mental calculation strategies. It stipulates in Year 4 that they should recognise and use factor pairs and commutativity in mental calculations and, in Year 5 that they use known facts. In Year 6, it simply says perform mental calcula-tion. All too often, the mental calculation aspect gets lost, and the formal written methods become the focus for division.

In Key Stage 2, we should be teaching division using arrays and manipulatives, such as place-value counters. Arrays help to deepen children's understanding of the relationship between multiplication and division. Children should have mastered division by the end of Year 5 so that in Year 6, the new learning would be dividing four-digit numbers by a two-digit divisor using either short or long division.

In Year 5, it specifically requires that children interpret remainders appropriately for the context. This is the first-time remainders appear in the national curriculum. However, interpreting them will be difficult for children if they have not experienced remainders before. Most numbers when dividing by a divisor will have remainders, so we should introduce them in Year 3 or even Year 2.

The following are examples of how we can help children gain a depth of understand-ing of division.

The following array shows that 18 multiplied by 6 equals 108 and that 6 multiplied by 18 equals 108. It also shows that 108 divided by 6 equals 18 and that 108 divided by 18 equals 6.

Diagram 4.18

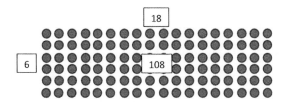

Using Dienes equipment or place-value counters really helps children to understand the formal written method.

Diagram 4.19

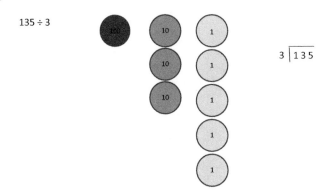

$135 \div 3$ means that we need to find how many groups of 3 we can make out of 135. We begin with 100. We cannot make a group of three 100s because there is only one. We therefore exchange the 100 for ten 10s.

Diagram 4.20

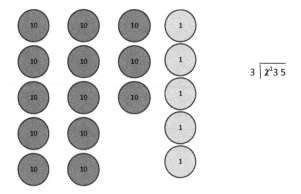

There are now thirteen 10s. We can make four groups of three 10s. There is one left over. We exchange the 10 for ten 1s.

Diagram 4.21

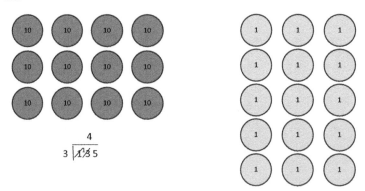

We can now make five groups of three 1s.

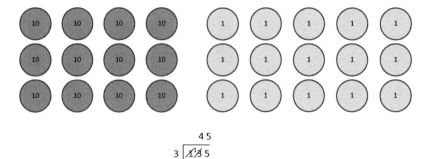

We should never refer to this as the 'bus stop' method. It is not a bus stop; it is the formal method for division, and the line enclosing the dividend is called the division bracket.

Scaling up and the link to ratio

Scaling up means that we make a number, amount or item larger, for example, twice as many, three times as many and four times the size. This is a child's first experience of ratio. In Year R, children double numbers. This is making something twice the size. So, scaling actually begins in Year R. We should be teaching this from Year 1 through simple problem solving with multiples of the numbers the children skip count. Scaling is mentioned in the national curriculum in Key Stage 2. It appears in the notes and guidance for measurement in Year 2, 'comparing measures includes simple multiples such as "half as high"; "twice as wide"'.

We should always expect the children to set scaling problems out using manipulatives such as counters or cubes. One counter or cube would represent the given amount in the problem. This would be placed above the counters showing how many times as many.

The following are some examples of scaling-up problems for number and measurement for each year group:

Year 1
Sammy had five marbles.
Toby had twice as many.
How many marbles did Toby have?
How many more marbles does Toby have?
How many marbles did they have altogether?

We, of course, need to add variation, so we could very the number of marbles and then the scale factor.

Sofia had 10 cm length of string.
Hannah had a piece three times as long.
How long was Hannah's piece?
How much longer is Hannah's?
What is the total length of both pieces of string?

Again, vary the length of string and the scale factor.

Year 2
Maisie had 12 cherries.
George had three times as many.
How many cherries did George have?
How many more cherries does George have?
How many do they have altogether?

Freddie had £3.
Maddy had four times as much.
How much money does Maddy have?
How much more money did Maddy have?
How much money did they have altogether?

For every two cars in the car park, there were three bikes.
If there were four cars, how many bikes were there?

Year 3

Joe had a collection of 45 stamps.
Michelle had a collection five times the size.
How many stamps did Michelle have?
How many more stamps did Michelle have?
How many stamps did they have altogether?

Samir had a strip of paper measuring 9.5 cm in length.
Flo had a strip of paper three times the length.
How long is Flo's strip of paper?
How much longer is Flo's strip?
What is the total length of the two strips?

For every two red tiles, there were three blue tiles.
If there were 12 red tiles, how many blue tiles were there?

Year 4

Natalie scored 236 points on a computer game.
Midge scored four times as many.
How many points did Midge score?
How many more points did Midge score?
How many points did they score altogether?

Alfie had a length of rope that measured 2.25 m.
Sam had a length three times as long.
How long was Sam's rope?
How much longer was Sam's rope?
How much rope did they have altogether?

For every three girls playing football, there were four boys.
If there were 21 girls playing football, how many boys were playing?

Year 5

Megan estimated that there were 1450 marbles in the jar.
Tim's estimate was three times more.
What was Tim's estimate?
How many more did Tim estimate?
What was the total of the two estimates?

Susie had a bottle of water containing a volume of 1.255 l.
Tommy had a bottle of water containing three times the volume.
What is the volume in Tommy's bottle?

How much more water did Tommy have?

What was the total volume of water?

For every four dresses in the clothes shop, there were five skirts.
If there were 36 dresses, how many skirts were there?

Year 6

There were 168,354 people at the football final.
There were three times as many people at the rugby final.
How many people were at the rugby final?
How many more people were at the rugby final?
How many people were at both finals?

Adam flew 2456 km to his holiday destination.
Lucy flew four times as far to hers.
How far did Amy fly?
How much farther did Amy fly?
What was the total distance they flew altogether?

For every four red flowers the gardener planted, he planted five white flowers.
If he planted 48 red flowers, how many white flowers did he plant?

Scaling down and the link to ratio

Scaling down is the inverse of scaling up. It means that we make a number, amount or item smaller, for example, half the size, one third as many or one fourth of the amount. Children begin this in Year R, when they halve numbers. As with scaling up, we should be teaching this from Year 1 through simple problem solving with the fractions the children have encountered. We should also expect the children to model what the problem looks like with counters or cubes.

The following are some examples of scaling-down problems for number and measurement for each year group.

Year 1

Sammy had 16 marbles.
Toby had half as many.
How many marbles did Toby have?
How many more marbles did Sammy have?
How many marbles did they have altogether?

Sofia had a 20 cm length of string.
Hannah had a piece one fourth of that length.
How long was Hannah's piece?
How much longer is Sofia's?
What is the total length of both pieces of string?

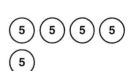

Year 2

Maisie had 24 cherries.
George had one third as many.
How many cherries did George have?
How many more cherries does Maisie have?
How many do they have altogether?

Freddie had £20.
Maddy had one fourth of that amount.
How much money does Maddy have?
How much more money did Freddie have?
How much money did they have altogether?

Year 3

Joe had a collection of 75 stamps.
Michelle had a collection one fifth of the size.
How many stamps did Michelle have?
How many more stamps did Joe have?
How many stamps did they have altogether?

Samir had a strip of paper measuring 30 cm in length.
Flo had a strip of paper one fourth of the length.
How long is Flo's strip of paper?
How much longer is Samir's strip?
What is the total length of the two strips?

Year 4

Natalie scored 426 points on a computer game.
Midge scored one third of Natalie's score.
How many points did Midge score?
How many more points did Natalie score?
How many points did they score altogether?

Alfie had a length of rope that measured 3 m.
Sam had a length one fourth of Alfie's length.
How long was Sam's rope?
How much longer was Alfie's rope?
How much rope did they have altogether?

Year 5

Megan estimated that there were 1458 marbles in the jar.
Tim's estimate was five sixths of Megan's.
What was Tim's estimate?
How many more did Megan estimate?
What was the total of the two estimates?

Susie had a bottle of water containing a volume of 1.5 l.
Tommy had a bottle of water containing one fifth of the volume.
What is the volume in Tommy's bottle?
How much more water did Susie have?
What was the total volume of water?

Year 6

There were 248,672 people at the football final.
There were five eighths of the number of people at the rugby final.
How many people were at the rugby final?
How many more people were at the football final?
How many people were at both finals?

Adam flew 2751 km to his holiday destination.
Lucy flew two thirds of that distance to hers.
How far did Amy fly?
How much farther did Adam fly?
What was the total distance they flew altogether?

Solving problems with multiplication and division

When the children have mastered the processes for multiplication and division, they can work on real word problems instead of worded scenarios! Word problems should be set so that the children have to think about what they need to do to find a solution. So mixing the two operations and asking problems that require both operations are helpful. Encourage them to use the bar model or draw pictures and diagrams, particularly for multiplication, so that they can see what to do more clearly.

Problems could include the following:

- Mr Smith had a delivery of tins of baked beans to his store.

  He put the tins on a shelf in six rows of 14.

  How many tins of beans were delivered?

  Mrs Smith came along and grouped the tins in groups of four.

  How many groups did she make?

- Megan works in a jewellery store.

  She was putting jewellery in display boxes.

  She had 125 rings and put 25 rings in each display box.

  How many display boxes did she use?

  Megan then sold 8 rings to a customer.

  Each one cost £32.45.

  How much did the customer pay?

- Mark had £168. He put his money into bags.

  He put £12 into each bag.

How many bags did he use?

He then took three of the bags and gave them to his sister.

How much money did he give his sister?

■ Mr Fox worked in a rope making factory.

Every hour, he produced 7 lengths of rope.

Each length was 75.5 m.

What was the total length of rope he made each hour?

What length does he make during his seven-hour working day?

■ Macy was cooking curry for a special dinner party.

She bought 720 g of curry powder.

She put 12 g of curry powder into each of her curries.

She used all the curry powder.

How many portions of curry did she make?

■ James had a container full of water.

Its volume was 45 l.

He decided to put the water into tubs.

He put 5 litres into each one.

How many tubs did he use?

His friend Tom took three of the tubs.

What volume of water did Tom take?

■ It took Sam 45 minutes to finish his homework.

It took Ella three times as long.

How many hours and minutes did it take Ella to finish her homework?

■ Freddie went for a hike.

It took him 5 hours.

He decided to have a break of 10 minutes every hour.

What was the total length of his breaks?

What was the total length of time he was hiking?

These types of problem can be asked of all children provided the numbers and contexts are adapted so that they are appropriate for a particular year group. Also, do not forget to add variation!

Solving problems with all four operations

In this country, we tend to teach addition and subtraction first and maybe follow this up with word problems. We then do the same for multiplication and division. It is usually in Year 6, when children explore problem solving using a mix of operations.

Higher-performing jurisdictions tend to use mixed operations much earlier in both calculations and word-problem solving.

Examples might include the following:

- Ruby had £10.

  She shared it equally between herself and a friend.

  Each of them spent £2.

  How much money was left?
- Bertie had £250.

  He is saving for a new bike. The bike cost £399.

  How much more does he need to save?

  He gets £3.50 pocket money a week.

  How long will it take him to save the rest of the money?
- Sam went to the shop. This is what he bought:

  5 tins of beans at 49 pence each, chicken £3.25, potatoes £1.50, 2 loaves of bread at £1.05 each and a box of chocolates.

  He spent £25. How much was the box of chocolates?
- The Blacks are planning a holiday. There are four in the family.

  They have saved £750 per person.

  The flights are £780 per person.

  The hotel costs £180 per night for the whole family.

  The Blacks are staying in the hotel for seven nights.

  How much more money do they need to save?

In Year 5, the measurement section of the national curriculum requires the children to understand and use approximate equivalences between metric units and common imperial units, such as inches, pounds and pints. In Year 6, they need to convert between miles and kilometres.

Using doubling, halving, adding, subtracting, multiplying and dividing by 10 encourages the children to use mental calculation strategies. Doubling and halving are the same as scaling up and scaling down.

For example, if we know the whole number fact that 5 mi = 8 km, we can use these strategies to work out many more facts:

- 5 mi = 8 km
- 10 mi = 16 km (by doubling/scaling up)
- 20 mi = 32 km (doubling/scaling up)
- 2.5 mi = 4 km (halving/scaling down)
- 1.25 mi = 2 km (halving/scaling down)

■ 15 mi = 24 km (adding 10 mi and 5 mi)

■ 7.5 mi = 12 km (adding 5 mi and 2.5 mi)

■ 17.5 mi = 28 km (subtracting 2.5 mi from 20 mi)

Although not in the national curriculum, another conversion children should explore is feet to metres. Children are often still measured in feet at home. If converting from feet to metres, we could use the same approach. One foot is 0.3048 m. We can round this to the nearest tenth to give an approximate equivalence of 0.3.

■ 1 ft ≈ 0.3 m

■ 2 ft ≈ 0.6 m (doubling/scaling up)

■ 4 ft ≈ 1.2 m (doubling/scaling up)

■ 0.5 ft ≈ 0.15 m (halving/scaling down)

■ 0.25 ft ≈ 0.075 m (halving/scaling down)

■ 2.5 ft ≈ 0.75 m (adding 2 ft and 0.5 ft)

■ 5 ft ≈ 1.5 m (adding 1 ft and 4 ft)

■ 3.5 ft ≈ 1.05 m (subtracting 0.5 ft from 4 ft)

The symbol ≈ means 'approximately', and we should introduce this symbol when we are giving approximate answers and not use the equal to symbol.

Other suggested imperial conversions to metric are inches, pounds and pints:

> 1 in. = 2.54 cm; we could round that to 2.5 cm.
> 1 cm = 0.393701 in.; we would round that to 0.4 in. or 0.39 in.
> 1 lb = 0.453592 kg; we would round that to 0.5 kg or 0.45 kg.
> 1 kg = 2.20462 lb; we would round to 2.2 lb.
> 1 pt = 0.568261 l; we would round this to 0.6 litre or 0.57 litre.
> 1 litre = 1.75975 pt; we would round this to 1.8 pt or 1.76 pt.

The links to decimals are obvious when we carry out activities such as these. It makes sense to include converting between units of measure to multiplication and division. These could be real life application activities, children carry out to practice skills involved in these two operations.

In the national curriculum, Year 6 children are required to calculate and interpret the mean as an average. This is new learning for them. This could be carried out during work on addition, subtraction, multiplication and division. These areas are taught together in Year 6, the idea being that they will have mastered the processes for all short-written methods in the years before and can therefore spend their time solving two-step and more than two-step problems in which they decide what they need to do to find the solution. Part of this problem solving could involve the mean as an average.

The average is a number expressing the central or typical value in a set of data. There are three types of average. All three used to be taught in the days of the NSS. These were the mode, the median and the mean. The mode is the most common value. The mean is the middle value in a list. The mean is the most common type of average which is calculated by dividing the sum of the values in the set by their number. This is also known as the central value.

For example, if we ask the children their shoe sizes and make a list of them, the list might look like this:

$$2 \quad 3 \quad 3 \quad 4 \quad 4 \quad 4 \quad 4 \quad 5 \quad 5 \quad 6$$

The most common size is 4; this is the mode.

The middle value is also 4; this is the median.

The mean is the sum of all the sizes, which is 36, divided by the number of sizes, which is 10. So, the mean is 3.6.

Sometimes all three are the same value. Sometimes they are different but usually quite close to each other.

A colleague of mine, Pip Huyton from Accomplish Education, shared a really good idea which could be used to introduce the concept of mean. The idea behind this is that the children work practically and do not need to add values and divide by the number of values at all. Doing this will give them a much better understanding of mean. After developing their understanding, they can then move onto the more abstract examples as mentioned earlier.

The children use interlocking cubes. Two children make two towers of different heights.

Diagram 4.22

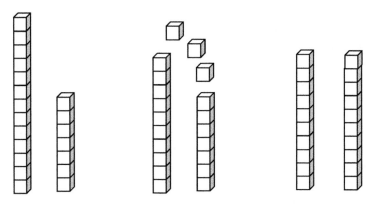

The tall tower is made from 13 cubes. The shorter one from seven. To find the mean, children can explore one of two ways. First, they could take cubes from the taller tower and add them to the shorter one until the two towers are of equal height. Adding three cubes will give two towers of the same height. We can now see that the central value or mean is 10.

An alternative method would be to make one long tower and halve it. This leads to the idea of adding the values and then dividing by the number of values.

You could then repeat this activity with three towers.

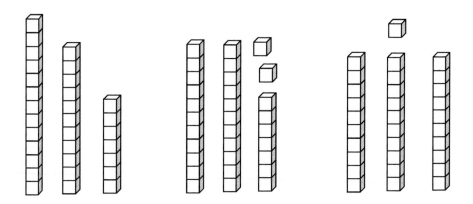

Again, the children attempt to make them equal as before.

Then they could make one tower and break it into three equal parts.

We can see in this example that there is one cube left over, so the mean would be between 10 and 11. By Year 6, most children should be able to tell you that the mean is 10 and one third, or approximately 10.3.

You could repeat this with four and then five towers. It is a great idea and a good way to help the children deepen their understanding of what mean is. It also enables them to develop the generalisation of how to find it, not just learn the rule.

Factors and multiples

In Year 5, children are required to identify multiples and factors, including finding all the factor pairs of a number and the common factors of two numbers. In Year 6, they need to identify common multiples and factors. We need to introduce the idea of factors and multiples before Year 5. We should be using this vocabulary from Year 3.

A multiple is the product of multiplying a number by another number.

Factors are numbers that are multiplied to get another number or the divisor or quotient of a dividend.

For example, 6 and 4 are factors of 24 because $6 \times 4 = 24$ and 24 is a multiple of both 6 and 4.

Children are often given activities in which they are given numbers and they have to find all their factors. Teaching them the divisibility rules as described earlier in this section makes a great deal of sense; this will make their task quicker and less laborious.

For example, consider 102. We know it is divisible by 2 because it is even. We know it is divisible by 3 and 6 because the digits' total is 3 and it is even. So, the factors are 1 and 102, 2 and 51, 3 and 34 and 6 and 17. If we know one factor, we divide by that factor to get its factor pair. A good way to do this is through partitioning as described in the mental calculation part of this section. For example, 102 can be partitioned into 60 and 42 to make dividing by 6 easier.

When we find the factors of two or more numbers, some factors might be the same. These are known as common factors. For example, 16 and 24, each have the common factors of 1, 2, 3 and 8.

A common multiple is a multiple of two or more numbers. For example, 12 and 24 are common multiples of three and four.

Making factor trees is fun. A factor tree is a special diagram which helps us find the factors of a number, then the factors of those numbers and so on until we cannot factor any more. We end up with prime factors, which is a requirement of the national curriculum.

Diagram 4.23

Here is an example:

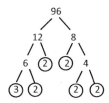

This tells us that $3 \times 2 \times 2 \times 2 \times 2 \times 2 = 96$.

Order of operations

In Year 6, children are required to use their knowledge of the order of operations to carry out calculations involving the four operations. We usually refer to this as BIDMAS or BODMAS.

BIDMAS stands for brackets, indices, division, multiplication, addition, subtraction.
BODMAS stands for brackets, orders, division, multiplication, addition, subtraction.

In both, division and multiplication rank equally, as do addition and subtraction.

This tells us how to add calculations with a mixture of operations. For example, with this calculation $(6 + 4) \times 7$, we need to carry out the addition first because it is in brackets: $10 \times 7 = 70$. In the calculation $6 + 4 \times 7$, there are no brackets so we do the multiplication first: $6 + 28 = 34$.

In this calculation $17 + 64 \div 2^2$, the squaring must be done first, then the division and finally the addition: $17 + 64 \div 4$ and $17 + 16 = 33$. If we did not have this order, we might add first $81 \div 2^2$ and then $81 \div 4 = 20.25$ – a completely different answer!

Year 6 is likely to be the first time that children will come upon this, so it is important that time is spent teaching and practising so that children consolidate and master this order.

Multiplying and links to perimeter

The measurement section of the national curriculum requires children in Year 4 to measure and calculate the perimeter of a rectilinear figure (including squares) in centimetres and metres.

The first thing that children need to understand is that the perimeter is the distance around a shape or an area. If they have been introduced to area in Key Stage 1 when looking at fractions, they should be able to tell you that area is the amount of space something takes up. Therefore, they should be able to tell you that the perimeter is the distance around an area.

It is a good idea to begin teaching children to find perimeters of rectangles starting with squares. They need to explore how they can do this and gradually develop the generalisation. They should be able to measure the length and notice that it is multiplied by 4, so we could say $l \times 4$ or $4l$.

Finding perimeters of oblongs involves a mixture of addition and multiplication. The children should explore the generalisation for this. They should be able to notice that they could add the length and width and double the sum, which would be $2(l + w)$. They could also double the length, double the width and add the two together, which would be or $2l + 2w$.

You could include other regular shapes. To find the perimeter of these, have children measure one side and multiply by the number of sides. For example, the perimeter of a pentagon would be $5l$; a hexagon, $6l$; and so on.

Square numbers and links to area

Children should be familiar with square numbers from learning their multiplication facts. A square number is a number multiplied by itself. There are 12 of them in the facts they need to learn by the end of Year 4.

In Year 5, children are required to recognise and use square numbers. If they have made the link to finding the areas of squares in Year 4, this should be straightforward.

In the measurement section of the national curriculum children in Year 4 are required to find the area of rectilinear shapes by counting squares Because they have looked at arrays when multiplying since Year 1 or 2, it makes sense to use their understanding of this to find the area of squares. They should not be counting squares to find areas of rectangles. Counting squares would be for shapes which are not rectangles.

Like arrays, grids similar to the one that follows, ideally with squares that have sides of 1 cm, should be used for multiplication because they are helpful for making the link between multiplication and finding areas of squares.

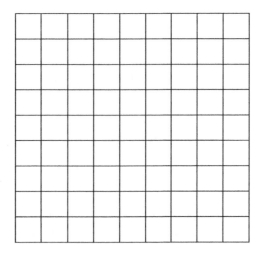

This is a nine-by-nine square. The calculation for finding the product or area is 9×9, or nine squared, which are both 81. When doing this in Year 4, we could introduce the notation 9^2.

The children should explore how to find the area in a quicker way than counting squares. They should be able to make the generalisation that to find the area of a square, they multiply the length by the width, or l × w. If using 1 cm squares, the children refer to the area as 81 cm².

After giving the children time to master this, we can move on to finding the area of oblongs. As earlier, children explore the generalisation of length multiplied by width.

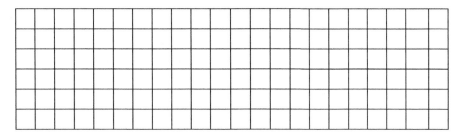

The area of this oblong is 22×7, which is 154 squares or, if using 1 cm squares, 154 cm².

Exploring the factors of square numbers is interesting. Can the children work out why square numbers have an odd number of factors and the other numbers have an even number of factors?

The following are square number examples:

- 16, factors are 1, 16, 2, 8 and 4, odd number of factors
- 25, factors are 1, 25 and 5, odd number of factors
- 36, factors are 1, 36, 2, 18, 3, 12, 4, 9 and 6, odd number of factors

Other number examples include the following:

- 15, factors are 1, 15, 3 and 5, even number of factors
- 18, factors are 1, 18, 2, 9, 3 and 6, even number of factors
- 39, factors are 1, 39, 3 and 13, even number of factors

The reason why there are an odd number of factors in square numbers is that one factor is always multiplied by itself to give a particular square number.

Cube numbers and links to volume

Children in Year 5 are required to recognise and use cube numbers and the notation for them. They are also required to estimate solid volume. Teaching cube numbers and volume of cubes together makes sense. Using interlocking cubes at first because these are easier to put together to make different-sized cubes is sensible. Eventually, they can use 1 cm cubes so that they can explore volumes of the standard unit of centimetres.

Diagram 4.24

This is a two-by-two-by-two cube. Its length, width and height are all two sides of the cubes. It has a volume of $2 \times 2 \times 2 = 8$ cubes and, eventually, when using 1 cm cubes, 8 cm³. We can link this to $2^3 = 8$. The children should be able to work the generalisation for finding the volume of cubes for themselves if given the opportunity to practically explore. They should notice that the volume can be found by multiplying the length, the width and the height ($l \times w \times h$).

After exploring the volume of cubes, they can find volumes of cuboids.

Diagram 4.25

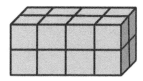

We should encourage them to explore whether the generalisation for finding the volume of cubes applies to cuboids. Sixteen cubes make up the volume of the pictured cuboid. The length is four, the width is two and the height is two, $4 \times 2 \times 2 = 16$, so the generalisation is the same.

Prime numbers

In Year 5, the children are required to know and use the vocabulary of prime numbers, prime factors and composite (non-prime) numbers. They have to establish whether a number up to 100 is prime and recall prime numbers up to 19.

In Year 6, they have to identify prime numbers, presumably to 100, as there is no fixed end number for this requirement.

A prime number is a number that is divisible by itself and one, so it has two factors. Two is the first prime number. One is not prime because it only has one factor, it is divisible by 1 only.

Exploring this on a 100 square is a good idea. Children could shade all the multiples of the numbers from 2 to 10. Of course, some of the first multiples will be prime because they are only divisible by 1 and the number, for example, 2, 3, 5 and 7. When they have done this, the prime numbers are obvious. They could do this using their knowledge of multiplication facts and also using some of the rules of divisibility. Other than 2, even numbers are not prime. Numbers with a digit total of 3, 6 and 9 will not be prime because they have at least three factors, 1, 3 and the number itself.

1	2	3	4	5	6	7	8	9	10
11	12	13	14	15	16	17	18	19	20
21	22	23	24	25	26	27	28	29	30
31	32	33	34	35	36	37	38	39	40
41	42	43	44	45	46	47	48	49	50
51	52	53	54	55	56	57	58	59	60
61	62	63	64	65	66	67	68	69	70
71	72	73	74	75	76	77	78	79	80
81	82	83	84	85	86	87	88	89	90
91	92	93	94	95	96	97	98	99	100

Using statistics to practise multiplication and division

Analysing data from pictograms and bar charts is a useful way to link statistics with multiplication. In a pictogram, each symbol should represent a different number of items.

Favourite flavour	Number of people
Chocolate	⬠⬠⬠⬠⬠⬠⬠⬠
Vanilla	⬠⬠⬠⬠⬠⬠
Strawberry	⬠⬠⬠⬠⬠⬠⬠⬠⬠
Pistachio	⬠⬠⬠⬠⬠⬠⬠⬠⬠⬠⬠
Toffee	⬠⬠⬠⬠⬠

⬠ represents 5 people.

To work out how many people chose each flavour, children would need to multiply the number of symbols by 5. Making the symbol represent any multiplication facts that the children are not fluent with is a good idea. Having appropriate shapes as symbols, for example, octagons for 8, is useful.

Once they have found out how many people voted for, in this case, ice creams, they can then answer questions that involve finding differences and totals.

You could ask the children to convert a pictogram into a frequency table to show, as in the previous example, how many people chose each flavour of ice cream.

You could then ask children to create their own pictograms with their own symbols representing a number and to ask questions about them.

Pictograms similar to this can be used throughout Key Stages 1 and 2; just adapt the numbers to suit the children.

For bar charts, similar activities can be developed.

The following bar chart shows the number of goals scored by four football teams over a season. The divisions are deliberately not labelled so that the teacher can decide what multiples they want the class to work on and so that the children can work out through multiplying what each division must be. If each division is worth 6, work with the children to add the correct numbers to position on the vertical axis.

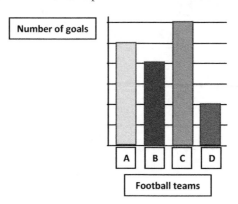

After finding the goals scored by each team, as with the pictogram example, children answer questions that involve finding totals and differences.

They could then make up their own bar charts with divisions increasing in multiples they choose and ask questions about it for a partner to answer.

Suggested progression for teaching multiplication and division

The following table sums up a suggested progression in multiplication and division that we are working on in some schools. I hope that you will find this helpful.

Year R	Doubling and halving; sharing with a link to fractions; count in steps of 1, 10, 5 and 2.
Year 1	Begin to develop mental calculation strategies, particularly those relating to commutativity and inverse and multiplication facts for 1, 2, 5 and 10; explore physical, pictorial and dotty arrays to introduce the concepts of multiplication as repeated addition and division as repeated subtraction; introduce the symbols for the two operations; simple scaling problems; sharing model for division linking to fractions.
Year 2	Continue to develop mental calculation strategies; consolidate multiplication and division facts for 1, 2, 5 and 10; increase counting in steps to 3 and 4 (double 2) and link to multiplication and division facts; explore multiplication and division using arrays; multiply by zero and 1; divide by 1; scaling problems; sharing model for division linking to fractions; introduce remainders.

Year 3	Rehearse and consolidate recall of multiplication and corresponding division facts from Year 2 and count in steps of 6, 12 and 8 and develop these facts, 6 is double 3 and 12 is double 6; look at patterns for these products; use partitioning as mental calculation strategy; multiply by 5 by multiplying by 10 and halving; divide by 5 by dividing by 10 and doubling; explore multiplication and division using arrays; move between arrays and the grid method for multiplication then introduce the column method; use manipulatives to explore division by taking groups of the divisor away from the dividend then practically introduce the written method; solve multiplication and division problems within the context of measurement; scaling problems; sharing model for division, linking to fractions; include remainders.
Year 4	Rehearse, consolidate and deepen mental calculation strategies to multiply and divide two- and three-digit numbers by a single digit; recall all multiplication facts to 12×12 and corresponding division facts; consolidate formal written methods for multiplication and division; solve problems involving multiplication and division within the context of measurement where children need to work out what to do; scaling problems; sharing model for division, linking to fractions; include remainders as fractions.
Year 5	Rehearse, consolidate and deepen mental calculation strategies to multiply and divide appropriate numbers, including numbers up to four digits; use formal written methods to multiply and divide numbers up to four digits by a single digit; multiply up to four digits by a two-digit number using a formal written method of long multiplication; solve problems involving multiplying and dividing within the context of measurement where children need to work out what to do; put remainders into context; scaling problems; sharing model for division, linking to fractions.
Year 6	Recap prior learning and continue to practise, consolidate and deepen within the context of measures, estimating and checking answers, using mental calculation strategies and written methods and solving problems; ratio and scaling problems; sharing model for division, linking to fractions

Reference

National Numeracy Strategy, Teaching mental calculation strategies guidance for teachers at key stages 1 and 2, https://www.stem.org.uk/elibrary/resource/29219, 1999.

5

Geometric reasoning

This section includes:

- Non-polyhedral shapes
- Polyhedral shapes
- Prisms
- Pyramids
- Triangles
- Platonic solids and other 3D shapes
- Polygons and non polygons
- Quadrilaterals
- Lines
- Symmetry
- Angles
- Position and direction
- Coordinates

Introduction

The national curriculum stipulates that children learn about the properties of two-dimensional (2D) and three-dimensional (3D) shapes. This suggests that teachers should begin with 2D shapes. I believe we should always introduce 3D shapes first as these will be the children's first experiences of shape. When they are very young, children will experience holding blocks, balls and other 3D shapes rather than looking at the 2D shapes around them. So, this is where we should begin. As we work with 3D shapes, we should explore the 2D properties of their faces with the children as an introduction to 2D shape.

Three-dimensional shapes have a length, a width and a height and an obvious link, as appropriate, to volume. Two-dimensional shapes have a length and a width and an obvious link, as appropriate, to perimeter and area.

The national curriculum also stipulates that children look at different elements of position and direction. For some reason, this is not in the requirements for Year 3; however, the requirement for understanding angles as the description of a turn in properties of 2D and 3D shapes can be regarded, to some extent, as position and direction.

Shape is one of those areas of the curriculum in which vocabulary is inconsistent. In this section, we explore the correct vocabulary to use for different elements of shape. My sources for the information on vocabulary include choice pieces found on the internet, for example, on the Maths Is Fun website (https://www.mathsisfun.com/) and books, such as Derek Haylock's *Mathematics Explained for Primary Teachers*. I have found that his book is a must-have for developing a teacher's subject knowledge. In the days when I was at the early stages of developing mine, I often looked at what he said about a variety of areas of mathematics. Happily, we agree on various points dealing with geometry – well, everything really!

In the Early Years Foundation Stage (EYFS), I encourage teachers to have a shape a week approach to this concept so that the children begin to gain a depth of understanding about the properties of each of those they study. From my experience, teachers often give the children a variety of 3D shapes to look at and to sort in whatever way they want. At this stage, children's sorting is very arbitrary. Generally, most children do not know enough about shapes to sort them according to any meaningful criteria. We need to give them the opportunity to explore the shapes and then ask them to sort selected shapes according to criteria that we initially give them and then criteria they can make up for themselves.

The shape a week idea has been very popular over the last few years, and many EYFS settings are embedding this idea into their curriculum plans. Year R teachers say that it is having an impact on the children's knowledge of shape and that they are gaining a deeper understanding.

Kerry and Helen from Georgian Gardens Primary School spent some time working on the shape a week approach, and this is what they say: 'With the thorough exposure to 3D and 2D shapes, children are confident to name and describe using correct mathematical language.'

Several years ago, when we were working together on planning a unit of work on shape, one teacher told me that she had carried out the shape a week approach in the autumn term. This was good because shape is one of the few areas in mathematics that does not need any understanding of counting and the prerequisites for numerical mathematical learning, so most four-year-olds can access it without prior knowledge of numbers. Children who find number work difficult can excel in shape activities. This teacher said that in the summer term, one girl came into class wearing a hat that she had made at home. This school has a tradition that EYFS children can wear a hat when it is their birthday. The little girl went straight to her teacher and said, 'Look at my hat; it is a cone shape, and this is its apex.' As she said this, she pointed to the apex of the cone. The teacher told me that this little girl was weak in other areas of mathematics, but she remembered this information about cones after nine months or so.

When working on shape in the Early Years, we could incorporate the language of position and direction. We could ask the children to position the shapes, for example, under a chair, on top of the table or between two other shapes. We could ask the children to move them in different directions, for example, to put a shape to the right of another shape or to roll a sphere forwards or backwards.

We will look at 3D and 2D shapes, beginning with what needs teaching in the EYFS and how this progresses into KS1 and KS2.

Non-polyhedral shapes

Non-polyhedral shapes are those that have curved surfaces, not faces. They include spheres, cylinders and cones. A face, by definition, is a flat or plane surface. We should therefore ensure that we describe the surfaces of non-polyhedral shapes as curved surfaces. Non-polyhedral shapes can also have curved or circular edges and sometimes circular faces. Each one commonly referred to in the primary classroom will be unpicked, and circles are explored when they are seen as the faces of some of these non-polyhedral shapes.

For each shape covered, displaying a selection of examples from real life and visual representations as well, for example, marbles for spheres, half an orange for hemispheres and a tin of beans for cylinders, is a good practice.

Sphere

A sphere is a shape that has one curved surface.

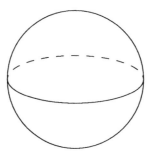

When teaching about spheres, particularly in the Early Years and Key Stage 1, it is important to have a collection of different sized spheres from everyday life, for example, oranges, marbles, tennis balls, table tennis balls or any soft balls you may have in the sports area of the school. In this way, they learn that a sphere is any shape with one curved surface and that the size does not matter.

It is common to hear young children referring to a sphere as 'Sophia' or 'spear'. I have heard it said, from an advisor who worked with special educational needs children, that the act of the children rolling plasticine or a similar malleable material into a sphere and saying the shape name work wonders. Very quickly, with the physical, visual, aural and oral coming together, children learn the correct pronunciation of the word *sphere*.

We must be sure to refer to a sphere as a shape with one curved surface and no other physical attributes; for example, it does not have edges or vertices.

One important property of a sphere is that it can roll. Apparently, a sphere will roll forever unless stopped by friction of any sort. This gives plenty of fun opportunities to explore the idea of rolling and the property that makes this possible. Throwing and catching, rolling and kicking competitions will help children become familiar with the properties of a sphere.

Hemisphere

A hemisphere is half a sphere. If we cut a sphere, for example, an orange, in half we create a hemisphere. A hemisphere has one curved surface, one circular edge and one circular face.

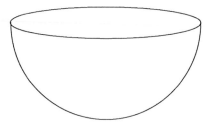

It can also roll. We could ask the children to compare the rolling property of a sphere with a hemisphere. A hemisphere has a limited rolling capacity; it can only roll from side to side.

Because it has a circular face, it can also slide. This gives children the opportunity to explore the difference between sliding and rolling and to discover the property needed for an object to slide. A shape has to have a face of some sort to slide.

Cylinder

A cylinder is a non-polyhedral shape that has one curved surface, two circular edges and two circular faces.

Contrary to some beliefs, a cylinder is not a prism. A prism, as shown later, is a shape that has two ends joined by rectangles which could be squares or oblongs.

A cylinder can roll and slide. We could ask the children to explore how a cylinder can roll and compare it with the rolling of a sphere and a hemisphere. They should notice that a cylinder rolls forwards or backwards in a straight line.

Cone

A cone has one curved surface, one circular edge, one circular face and one apex. We should not call the pointed part of the cone a vertex. By definition, a vertex is made by the joining of edges.

It can roll in circles. Again, children could explore the way this shape rolls and explore the differences in the way a sphere, a hemisphere, a cylinder and a cone roll. It can also slide.

Circles

When exploring hemispheres, cylinders and cones, we have the perfect opportunity to introduce the 2D shape of a circle. When looking at a circular face of these shapes, we can see that a circle has one continuous edge with no start or finish point. Circles, as 2D shapes, in their own right, do not have one edge. They actually have an infinite number of edges. A circle is created by an infinite number of radii emanating from a central point. This is interesting to explore with older children. We could ask them to draw a circle by drawing radii and then joining the end points of the radii. I always give them squared paper to do this on because it makes drawing the radii simpler.

Diagram 5.1

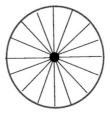

There are websites, notably Geogebra (https://www.geogebra.org), that show how a circle is formed. The children can find this fascinating. We should therefore not tell children that a circle has one side because it does not.

Young children could draw around the circular edges of a variety of different-sized hemispheres, cylinders and cones so that they can see that a circle is a circle no matter what size it is. Hemispheres and cones are easier for them to draw around. Alternatively, they could make prints by stamping these shapes in paint and printing onto paper. Doing so would make an interesting display.

Older children could explore concentric circles. Concentric circles are circles with a common centre point. The space between the edges of two concentric circles is called the annulus. Children could make concentric circles by dropping coins or stones into a bowl of water.

Diagram 5.2

In Year 6, children are required to illustrate and name parts of circles, including the radius, the diameter and the circumference. They are expected to know that the diameter is twice the radius. Other parts of a circle that children will learn about later in their education are, for example, chord (line), sector and segment (section).

They could also investigate the length of the circumference of a circle and make the link that the circumference is roughly three times the diameter. A good way to do this is to take a piece of string, place it around the circular edge of a cylindrical tin and cut it when it is the same as the circumference. Children measure the length of the string and compare it to the length of the diameter of the tin.

Children also need to know that half a circle is called a semicircle.

Torus

Even though this is not in the requirements of the national curriculum, exploring the properties of a torus is fun. A torus is the same shape as a rubber ring that some children use when they learn to swim. It is the same shape as a doughnut with a hole in the middle and a hoop.

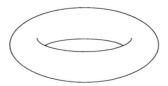

It has one curved surface and therefore can roll. You could ask the children to find out how far they can roll a hoop.

Polyhedral shapes

Polyhedral shapes have faces, edges and vertices. Edges appear where faces meet, and vertices appear where edges meet. Children need to be aware of this as soon as they begin to look at polyhedrons.

Polyhedral shapes include prisms and pyramids, which are typically looked at in the primary curriculum. They also include platonic solids and other shapes made up from, often, a mixture of different polygons. These are looked at later in this section. First those shapes typically covered in primary school are considered, and links to the 2D shapes which make up their faces are made.

As for non-polyhedral shapes, having a selection of examples of shapes from real life and visual representations of each shape that is covered, for example, dice for cubes and cereal boxes for cuboids, is good practice.

Cube

A cube is a platonic solid because it is made with regular quadrilaterals, namely squares. A cube has 6 faces, all squares; 12 edges; and 8 vertices. It is a prism because its square end faces are joined by regular rectangles which are squares.

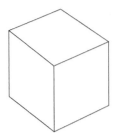

Cuboid

Cuboids have the same properties as cubes: 6 faces, 12 edges and 8 vertices. This means that a cube is a special type of cuboid. The national curriculum refers to cuboids, including cubes in the geometry section. Cuboids are also prisms; their end faces are joined by rectangles, which are oblongs. The difference between cubes and cuboids is the shape of their faces. Cuboids could have six oblong faces or two square and four oblong faces.

Rectangles

When exploring cubes and cuboids, there is an obvious link to rectangles which form the faces of these 3D shapes. The definition of a rectangle is any four-sided shape with four right angles. There are two types: regular and irregular. A regular rectangle is a square, and an irregular one is an oblong. The word *oblong* comes and goes in our mathematical vocabulary. It was there in the days of the National Numeracy Strategy (NSS). It seems to have gone out of fashion now. I believe *oblong* should be there permanently so that we can differentiate between the two types of rectangle. I have heard a lot of children in all year groups up to Year 6 say that a square is not a rectangle when it is. They seem to believe squares and rectangles are different shapes.

Prisms

As mentioned previously, a prism, by definition, has end faces joined by rectangles which can be both squares or oblongs. We need to give the children opportunities to explore a variety of these. Cubes and cuboids have already been discussed. Children need to explore the properties of other prisms. Triangular prisms are a good example, as are pentagonal and hexagonal prisms. Triangular prisms have two triangular faces joined by three rectangular faces. They have a total of five faces, nine edges and six vertices. Pentagonal prisms have two pentagonal faces joined by five rectangular faces. They have a total of 7 faces, 15 edges and 10 vertices. Hexagonal prisms have two hexagonal faces joined by six rectangular faces. They have a total of 8 faces, 18 edges and 12 vertices.

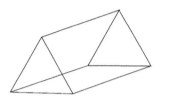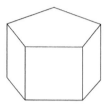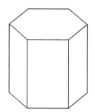

There are many potential prisms because there are many potential end-shaped faces.

Older children should be given the opportunity to figure out the generalisation for the number of faces, edges and vertices of a prism. The following table shows how we can build up to doing this.

Table of prisms

Shape	Faces	Edges	Vertices
Triangular prism	5	9	6
Cube	6	12	8
Pentagonal prism	7	15	10
Hexagonal prism	8	18	12

Of course, children explore for themselves using the shapes in the table, either ones they make or are given. From their exploration they should be able to say how many faces, edges and vertices they have. They complete a table such as the one above. They can then explore the patterns made. If we look at the vertical pattern, we can see that the number of faces increases by one, the number of edges by three and the number of vertices by two. The vertical pattern does not help us make the generalisation. For this, we need to look at the horizontal pattern. The faces are always two more than the number of sides the named shape has. The edges are always three times the number of sides the named shape has. The number of vertices is always double the number of sides the named shape has.

The generalisation is therefore $n + 2$ for faces, $3n$ for edges and $2n$ for vertices, where n is the number of sides the shape making the ends has. We can then use this to find the number of faces, edges and vertices for every prism.

Prisms are easy shapes to make, and children should be given the opportunity to work out what their nets would look like by examining the actual shapes. They should then sketch the net, cut it out and fold it. It will not be perfect, but the children will have made a reasonable example. They then make a measured example and fold it to construct a more accurate prism. This is a good visualisation activity, and we need to give the children plenty of opportunities to develop this skill.

The following are possible nets for each of the prisms mentioned. In each you can see the end faces and the rectangles that join them. These are not the only nets. Asking some children to explore alternative nets as an extension is good.

Diagram 5.3

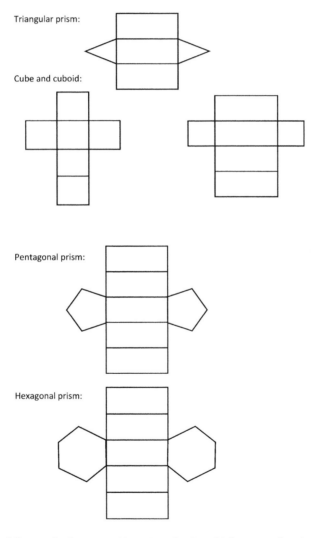

I have successfully taught lessons in Years 5 and 6 in which we explored wooden prisms and then the children made their own and worked out the generalisation for finding the numbers of faces, edges and vertices of any prism.

Making nets is a requirement for Year 6. In my experience, much younger children can do this, and waiting until making nets is required before we let them carry out shape investigations such as this is a shame. From my experience, the square-based pyramid is the simplest one for the children to visualise. This is considered later.

When looking at prisms, there are opportunities to explore the 2D shapes of triangles, pentagons and hexagons. These are looked at in more depth later.

Pyramids

Pyramids have a base and then, depending on the shape of the base, a different number of triangular faces. The one with the least number of faces is the triangular pyramid, which is called a tetrahedron, a word that we need to introduce the children to. It has a triangular base and three other triangular faces, making a total of four faces. The triangular faces are equilateral triangles. It also has six edges and four vertices. A tetrahedron is also a platonic solid (see next part of this section).

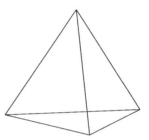

When placing a tetrahedron, and any other pyramid, on its base, the top vertex is also called an apex. The apex is the farthest point from the base of an object. In primary school, we generally call the apex a vertex. We should also introduce the vocabulary of *apex* and explain what one is.

The next pyramid is a square-based pyramid. This has a square base and four triangular faces joined to the base; it has a total of five faces, eight edges and five vertices or four vertices and one apex.

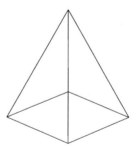

The pentagonal-based pyramid has a pentagonal base and five triangular faces coming from the base, making a total of six faces. It also has 10 edges and 6 vertices or 5 vertices and 1 apex.

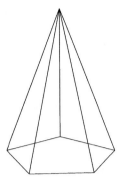

Another commonly explored pyramid is the hexagonal-based pyramid. It has a hexagonal base and six triangular faces joining the base, making a total of seven faces. It also has 12 faces and 7 vertices or 6 vertices and 1 apex.

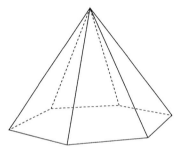

There are many potential pyramids because there are many potential base shapes.

As with prisms, older children should be given the opportunity to find the generalisation for the number of faces, edges and vertices of a pyramid. The following table shows how we can build up to doing this.

Table of pyramids

Shape	Faces	Edges	Vertices
Triangular based pyramid	4	6	4
Square based pyramid	5	8	5
Pentagonal based pyramid	6	10	6
Hexagonal based pyramid	7	12	7

If we look at the vertical pattern, we can see that the number of faces increases by one, the number of edges by two and the number of vertices by one. As with prisms, the vertical pattern does not help us make the generalisation. For this, we need to look at the horizontal pattern. The faces are always one more than the number of sides the base shape has. The edges are always double the number of sides the base shape has. The number of vertices is always one more than the number of sides the base shape has.

So the generalisation for the number of faces is $n + 1$, edges are $2n$ and the vertices are $n + 1$, where n is the number of sides the base shape has. This is a great link to algebra. We should always be on the lookout for links to algebra, and shape is one of those topics that gives opportunities for this.

As with prisms, asking the children to visualise what pyramids would look like if opened up is good practice. Whenever I teach shape, we do this in all years in Key Stage 2. We start with a square-based pyramid as it is the simplest to visualise opened up. The children visualise what they would see if they peeled the triangular faces back and down – a little like peeling a banana! They then sketch what they see, cut it out and fold it to see if it works. We then discuss how their nets could be improved. We agree that the base must be square and that the triangles that will make the faces must be exactly the same size. Then I give the children squared paper and rulers and ask them to make an accurate one. Guiding this activity by giving specific instructions about the size of the square and the height of the triangles often makes it more successful. This works really well.

These nets are of commonly taught pyramids. As with prisms, there are alternative nets, and letting children explore what these might be a good activity.

Diagram 5.4

Triangular pyramid:

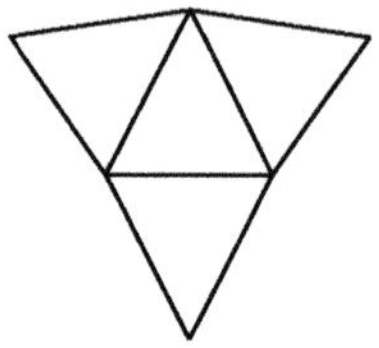

Square-based pyramid:

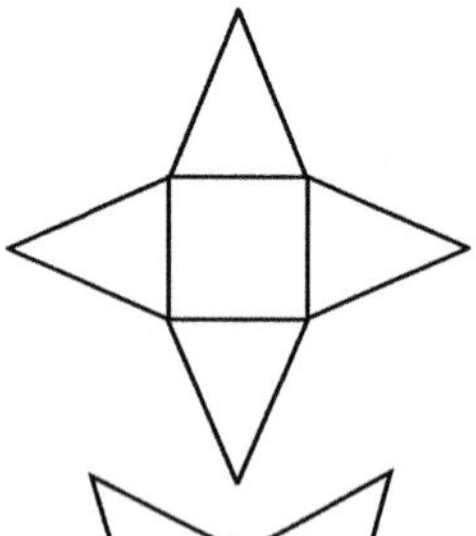

Pentagonal-based pyramid:

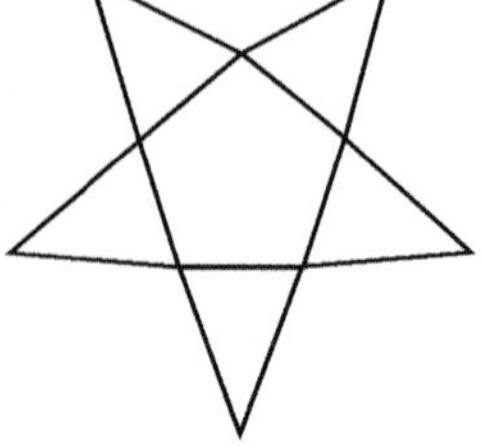

Hexagonal-based pyramid:

Triangles

Of course, working on pyramids gives an ideal opportunity for studying triangles. Children should make the generalisation that any three-sided shape is a triangle from the Early Years. It does not have to be an equilateral triangle, which is often how young children see them. We need to show them lots of different triangles in different orientations so that they do not develop misconceptions. There is no such thing as an upside-down triangle!

The national curriculum seems to imply that going more in-depth with these shapes is not necessary until Year 4 when it is required. Personally, I think we need to begin naming triangles in earlier years so that children become familiar with the names that they need to learn. Children should be given the opportunity to sketch different triangles on plain paper. These do not necessarily have to be accurately constructed at this stage. We are trying to help children understand that triangles can look different.

There are three types of triangle. These are equilateral, isosceles and scalene. Some people talk about right-angled triangles. These are not really a classification because isosceles and scalene triangles can have right angles. When these arise, we could call them right-angled isosceles triangles and right-angled scalene triangles.

An equilateral triangle has three sides which are equal length and three angles, vertices or corners that are the same size. A school being consistent in its use of *corners* or *vertices* for the point where two lines meet is important. For children to know that both are correct is helpful.

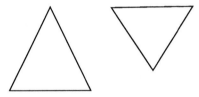

An isosceles triangle has two sides that are the same length and two angles, vertices or corners that are equal. One side is a different length from the other two, and one angle is different from the other two angles.

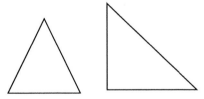

A scalene triangle is a triangle where all sides are different lengths and all angles, vertices or corners are different sizes.

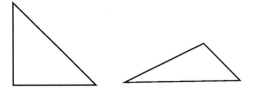

The national curriculum expects children in Year 1 to recognise and name common 3D shapes. This should be done very practically with wooden or plastic shapes and shapes within real-life contexts. They need to develop an understanding of their properties as discussed earlier, including whether they can roll and/or slide.

For Year 2, the national curriculum expects the children to describe shapes in terms of numbers of faces, edges and vertices. Including the correct vocabulary from the beginning is good practice, so Year R children should be familiar with these terms, Year 1 should use them and by Year 2 these should be used confidently whenever appropriate. They are also expected to identify the 2D shapes of the 3D shape's faces, which should be common practice from the beginning when starting to explore 3D shapes. They need to compare and sort common 3D shapes and everyday items.

In Year 3, children are required to make 3D shapes using modelling materials and recognise and describe 3D shapes in different orientations. I would add here that they could begin to explore nets as previously described for square-based pyramids. By now, children should be exploring a variety of prisms and pyramids.

My favourite activity in Key Stage 2 is a plasticine one. Each child has a piece of this or another malleable substance. I ask them to make a sphere and describe its properties and what they would see in the real world that looks like this. I then ask them to change their sphere into a cube and to describe what they are doing: flattening the sphere's curved surface to make faces. We then talk about the cube's properties and where this shape would be found in real life. They then turn the cube into a cuboid and talk about what they do. Are they changing the number of faces, edges and vertices? They know that they are not, but they are changing the shape of the faces, making at least four oblongs. I then ask them to make a square-based pyramid. Many can find this tricky, but with perseverance, they usually make a reasonable one. Any adults watching will help the few who really struggle. Again, we discuss its properties, where they can see these in real life, and then the making of the net begins. I ask them to put the square base on the table and look on top. They imagine that they are pulling the triangular faces out and down. Then we continue as described previously. The whole activity is a great one to do; it has the physical and visual attributes that help children learn.

There are no requirements in Year 4 for 3D shape. However, if we do not revise the names and properties of 3D shapes in Year 4 and simply leave it until Year 5, many children will forget. Geometry has far less curriculum time spent on it than number-related topics, so when we teach it, our lessons need to be engaging and effective. As teachers, we need to ensure that we plan at least one week of work on 3D shapes, linking this with the shape's 2D faces and, as appropriate, moving into other aspects of 2D shape. For example, when looking at rectangles in prisms, we can then more specifically work on the different quadrilaterals, which is an expectation of the Year 4 curriculum. We discuss these later in this section.

I would repeat the plasticine activity done in Year 3 for Year 4. The children really enjoy it and will learn something new if they do it again. I would extend the making, visualising and net idea to a variety of pyramids and prisms. Triangular prisms are a straight forward shape to make. Initially, their nets are easier to visualise than are those of cubes and cuboids.

In Year 5, children are expected to identify 3D shapes, including cubes and other cuboids, from 2D representations. They should have mastered this by now, so we need to enrich their shape offering by exploring different shapes such as platonic solids and others which are mentioned later.

According to the national curriculum Year 6 children need to recognise, describe and build simple 3D shapes, including making nets. They should be able to make nets, if the preceding activities have been followed, which is a good thing, because they have other new learning in geometry and not very much time to master it. They will also need to revise all shape work from Years 3 through to Year 5 for their standard assessment test. The more children have mastered through a sensible progression and plenty of consolidation, the less they need to learn in Year 6, and so 3D shape work will simply be revision.

Platonic solids and other 3D shapes

Primary geometry tends to focus on the types of shape previously mentioned, mostly prisms and pyramids, as well as non-polyhedral shapes. However, there are other 3D shapes do not fall into these categories. Three of the five platonic solids are an example. A cube and a tetrahedron are both platonic solids, which are usually covered in the primary curriculum, cubes certainly are. A cube is a prism, and a tetrahedron is a pyramid. The other three platonic solids do not fall into the prism and pyramid classifications. These are the octahedron, dodecahedron and icosahedron. Platonic solids are 3D shapes that have regular polygon faces with the same number of faces meeting at each vertex. These five shapes are the only ones that meet that criterion. An octahedron has 8 faces that are equilateral triangles, 12 edges and 6 vertices. It looks very much like two square-based pyramids that have been stuck together base on base. A dodecahedron has 12 regular pentagonal faces, 30 edges and 20 vertices. An icosahedron has 20 faces in the shape of equilateral triangles, 30 edges and 12 vertices. It has five of its equilateral triangles meeting at each vertex.

You can find nets of these shapes easily on the internet, and exploring these is a fun addition to the usual shape activities we carry out. These are not included in the national curriculum requirements but are worth investigating.

Another shape that the children will be very familiar with is the one that looks like a football. It is made up of a mixture of pentagonal and hexagonal faces. It is called a probate spheroid or a truncated icosahedron. It is shaped the way it is because it is also the shape of an inflated pig's bladder, which is what the first footballs were made of. It is probably not necessary to share this with the children unless you want to, but showing them shapes other than the usual ones that we teach them about is a good idea.

A couple people have done some interesting work with 3D shapes, and they are worth exploring for your own interest, if not to explore with the children. One, an American, Richard Buckminster Fuller, is famous for his work on geodesic domes. These are hemispherical shell-like structures made from equilateral triangles. They can hold a surprising amount of mass. It is worth exploring his work and creating some activities for the children based on geodesic domes that would link mathematics with some science.

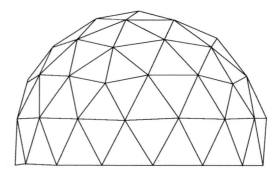

Another person worthy of note is a Polish gentleman, Wacław Franciszek Sierpinski. He is well known for his interesting tetrahedrons and triangles. Again, although not a requirement of the national curriculum, making these is good fun and makes great displays for art. I have done work with the children on his triangles and tetrahedrons. The tetrahedrons were tricky!

You could try this Sierpinski activity with Key Stage 2 children:

- Ask the children to draw an equilateral triangle.
- They then make another but at half its height and base.
- They stick the new triangle in the middle of the original triangle.
- They then repeat this as many times as you want them to, making an arrangement similar to the one that follows.

You could use this idea to explore area, fractions and percentages; for example, 'What fraction/area/percentage of the large triangle is this smaller triangle?' One thing is certain: it could make a really interesting and colourful display for your classroom.

It is worth letting children, who are confident with the shape requirements that they need to master, play around with the more advanced ideas of these two men.

Polygons and non polygons

There are essentially two types of 2D shapes: polygons and those that are not polygons.

A polygon is any 2D shape formed with straight sides. Triangles, quadrilaterals, pentagons and hexagons are all examples of polygons. The name tells you how many sides the shape has.

As discussed, when we looked at circles, a circle is considered to be a polygon with an infinite number of sides. However, in the primary curriculum, circles are considered not to be polygons. Other examples are ellipses and shapes that have a mixture of straight and curved sides, such as a semicircle. The following are some shapes that are not polygons.

Diagram 5.5

As mentioned, the name of the shape tells us how many sides it has. The *–agon* suffix for all our shapes is from the Greek word that means 'angle', so, for example, hexagon is a shape with six angles.

We should be encouraging children to make generalisations from Year R:

- Any three-sided shape is a triangle.
- Any four-sided shape is a quadrilateral. The national curriculum does not mention the word *quadrilateral* until the requirements for Year 4. In previous years, the word *rectangles*, including squares, is the only reference to four-sided shapes. Children need to know that any four-sided shape is a quadrilateral from the beginning of their work in geometry.
- Any five-sided shape is a pentagon.
- Any six-sided shape is a hexagon.
- Any seven-sided shape is commonly called a heptagon. Some people refer to it as a septagon. *Septagon* is from a Latin word, where *sept* means 'seven'. *Heptagon* is from a Greek word, where the *epta* part of the word means 'seven'.
- Any eight-sided shape is an octagon.
- Any nine-sided shape is a nonagon. This comes from the Latin word *nonus*, which means 'ninth'.
- Any 10-sided shape is a decagon.
- Any 11-sided shape is a hendecagon or undecagon. The name *hendecagon* comes from Greek word *hendeka* which means 'eleven'. *Undecagon* comes from the Latin word *undecim*, which also means 'eleven'.
- Any 12-sided shape is a dodecagon.

I like to name all shapes up to the dodecagon because this is the shape of the end faces of the prism which is our pound coin. We can keep going because every shape has a name, but I think that in general primary teaching, we need to draw the line somewhere!

One important aspect of polygons is that there are two types of each. There is only one regular polygon for each shape. Regular shapes have equal lengths of sides and equal angles. There are many irregular versions for each shape. Irregular shapes need to have the correct number of sides and angles, but these can all be different or a mixture of the same and different. For example, an isosceles triangle is irregular with two sides and angles the same and one side and one angle that are different.

Quadrilaterals

As we know, any four-sided shape is a quadrilateral. Some quadrilaterals have special names and properties. Year 4 are expected to start exploring these.

We have previously discussed rectangles as quadrilaterals with four right angles. Regular rectangles are squares, and irregular rectangles are oblongs.

Diagram 5.6

Children also need to learn about the following quadrilaterals:

- The parallelogram: a quadrilateral with two pairs of parallel sides. A parallelogram includes both types of rectangle.

- The rhombus: a parallelogram with four equal sides and the opposite angles are equal. The diagonals of a rhombus are perpendicular; they bisect at right angles. A square is a rhombus. Sometimes, books and teachers refer to a rhombus, such as the one that follows, as a diamond. There is no such shape as a diamond!

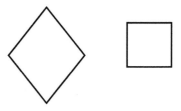

- The trapezium: a quadrilateral with one pair of parallel sides

- The kite: a quadrilateral with two pairs of equal adjacent sides. The diagonals of a kite are perpendicular. Angles between unequal sides are equal. A rhombus is also a kite; so is a square. We can generally say that any quadrilateral that has perpendicular diagonals, one of which is a line of symmetry, is a kite.

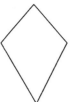

In Year 2, children are required to identify and describe the properties of 2D shapes, including the number of sides and line symmetry in a vertical line. Symmetry now appears as a property of shape. We look at symmetry shortly.

Children are also expected to compare and sort common 2D shapes and everyday objects. Carroll and Venn diagrams are not mentioned in the national curriculum. However, these diagrams are great for sorting shape, highlighting, for example, one criterion and showing shapes that do and do not meet that criterion.

Quadrilaterals	Not quadrilaterals
Examples: Parallelogram Square Kite Rhombus	Examples: Triangle Pentagon Hexagon Octagon

In Year 3, children are required to draw 2D shapes. It is important that they draw irregular and regular shapes.

In Year 4, children are required to compare and classify geometric shapes, including quadrilaterals and triangles, based on their properties and sizes.

In Year 5, children are required to identify 3D shapes from 2D representations. If they have mastered 3D shape, this is a fairly straightforward expectation.

In Year 6, children are required to draw 2D shapes using given dimensions and angles. This means that they need to have a good understanding of angles. Angles are looked at in more depth later.

Just a Minute is a good game to play to reinforce the vocabulary of shape.

I give groups of four mixed attainment children a pack of individually cut out cards similar to those that follow.

square	oblong	rectangle	triangle	circle
pentagon	hexagon	octagon	pyramid	cube
cone	face	cuboid	corner	cylinder
sphere	vertex	trapezium	edge	apex

I choose the most confident child to begin. This child takes one card at a time and describes the word they see. The rest of the group has to guess the word. When they guess correctly, the first child places the card face-up on the table so that the word is showing. Doing this is helpful for visual learners. They are timed for a minute. At the end of the minute, they count the number of words that they guessed correctly. They put the guessed words on the top of the pack so that these words appear first, and most children will remember them. Then the next most confident child repeats the process for another minute. A few more cards will be guessed correctly. They do this four times in total so that every child has a chance to describe and to guess. The fourth child, who may be the least confident, has heard three descriptions and will have a bank of words to help him or her describe the words during his or her turn. Usually, the number of words guessed has increased at the end of the fourth child's turn. It is a great activity, and the children enjoy it immensely.

Barrier games are also a great idea for improving vocabulary. The children work in pairs, and for example, child A has a 2D or 3D shape that child B does not know. In a barrier game, child A and child B sit with a barrier between them, and child A is required to convey information about his or her shape, without naming it, for child B to identify.

In our teaching of geometry, we need to look out for opportunities for investigation. The NRICH website (https://nrich.maths.org/) has some good ideas.

A good investigation to carry out is one using a seven-piece tangram. Ask children to work in pairs to put the pieces together to make a square. Give them a few minutes to experiment. When a pair of children have made the square, they have to describe where they put each shape to make it. That task is quite challenging, but it is useful for encouraging mathematics talk and positional vocabulary. You could then ask the children to make a triangle and then explore the other shapes that they can make. They should draw and name the shapes that they make.

Diagram 5.7

A famous investigation is the pentominoes investigation.

Introduce this by showing a domino pattern made up of two squares.

Move onto triominoes, patterns made up of three squares.

Then introduce tetrominoes, patterns made up of four squares.

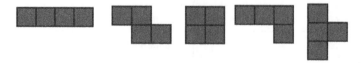

The children's task is to find all the patterns they can with five squares (pentominoes).

I have seen this done in Year 1, where the children worked with a partner using five large squares so that they can manipulate them to make their new shapes. They then copy those they make onto squared paper.

In Key Stage 2, I generally give them squared paper to draw their shapes. The pentominoes have to be different, no reflections or rotations. There are 12 altogether.

Diagram 5.8

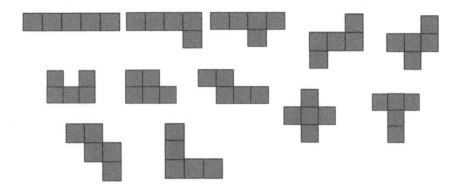

When the children have found and drawn these, they should label them with their shape names. They could identify the number of lines of symmetry each shape has.

You could ask them to cut their shapes out and to use them to make reflections. They could also work out how to fit them together to make an oblong.

Lines

In geometry, a line is straight, it has no thickness and it extends in both directions infinitely. When we make a beginning and an end to a line, we create a line segment. This concept is concept and worth mentioning to children when they begin to look at perpendicular and parallel lines.

The requirements for a more in-depth understanding of lines begins in Year 3, when children need to identify horizontal and vertical lines and pairs of perpendicular and parallel lines. If following the number of the week idea, children will be familiar with *horizontal* and *vertical* from the individual lines that appear in the number 1.

They need to know that perpendicular lines form a right angle. Children have been exploring rectangles for some time and so should be able to make the connection between rectangles and perpendicular and parallel lines quite easily.

There is no specific mention of diagonal lines, but these could be included, particularly when looking at the diagonals in quadrilaterals to identify a square, a rhombus and a kite.

Symmetry

Symmetry makes an appearance in Years 2 and 4. In Year 2, they simply identify whether a shape is symmetrical or not with a vertical line. They should continue to do this in Year 3 but in both vertical and horizontal lines. It would also be worth exploring diagonal lines of symmetry. Symmetry is extended further in Year 4 when they identify lines of symmetry in a 2D shape presented in different orientations.

There is no reference to symmetry in Years 5 and 6, but we must ensure that we continue to cover this area when looking at 2D shapes so that they do not forget what symmetry is. The word used for these year groups is *reflection*. In earlier years, they identify symmetry in 2D shapes. Year 4 are required to do both this and begin to explore reflection, although this word is not used. The requirement is that they need to be able to complete a simple symmetric figure across a specific line of symmetry, which is the start of reflection. A classic activity for this is to give the children, for example, half of a symmetrical picture or a face. They stick this on half a piece of plain paper, and they draw the other half on the other half of the paper.

In Year 5, children need to identify, describe and represent the position of a shape after a reflection, presumably across a specific line of symmetry. The notes and guidance suggest they also do this when looking at coordinates. In Year 6, they should reflect shapes across an axis when looking at coordinates.

Children need to know that for a shape or picture to be symmetrical one half must be identical to the other half. They only need to learn about the simplest type of symmetry which is reflection. We often call the line of symmetry the mirror line, and some teachers give the children mirrors to explore whether shapes or pictures are symmetrical.

We used to teach rotational symmetry, which is trickier, but that is no longer a primary requirement. Rotational symmetry is when an image is rotated around a central point so that it appears at least two times. The number of times it appears is called the order.

Angles

Angles are quite a focus in the national curriculum, and it is important that we teach these properly.

There are two types of angle that we need to teach the children about. One is static, which is a measure of the space between two lines that meet at a point, corner or vertex. The other is dynamic, which is recognising the size of an angle as the amount of turn between the straight lines.

The International System of units measures the size of an angle in a unit called radian. This is the point between two radii of a circle; see shown in the following diagram. In this country, we use degrees, indicated by a small circle:°. Degrees are an internationally accepted measurement.

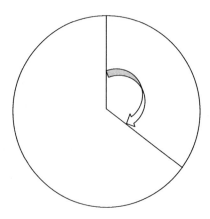

In Year 3, children need to recognise angles as a property of shape or a description of a turn. They need to identify right angles, which, it could be argued should have been started in Year R. The suggestions for number of the week encourages this for the number 2 when the horizontal and vertical lines from the number one are put together. Some verbal feedback that I have given about this is that the children in Year R can now point out right angles everywhere. More information on this can be found in the Number Sense section of this book.

Year 3 children should also recognise that two right angles make a half turn, three make three quarters of a turn and four a complete turn. They should be able to identify whether angles are greater than or less than a right angle. The curriculum does not mention naming angles as acute, obtuse or reflex; however, introducing these terms as they are identified seems sensible. *Acute* is the word for angles smaller than 90°, *obtuse* describes angles that are between 90° and 180° and *reflex* is used for angles greater than 180°. A reflex angle is the angle outside a right, acute or obtuse angle. When together, they make a circle.

In Year 4, children are expected to identify acute and obtuse angles and compare and order the size of two angles up to 180°. The argument here would be that *acute* and *obtuse* should be introduced in Year 3 when the children identify angles that are smaller than 90° and between 90° and 180°. So Year 4 children could extend this to reflex angles.

There are a lot of requirements for angles in Year 5, so the more we can help children be ready for this before they start in this year, the better and naming the angles is one thing that is achievable.

- know angles are measured in degrees: estimate and compare acute, obtuse and reflex angles
- draw given angles, and measure them in degrees (°)
- identify
  - angles at a point and one whole turn (total 360°)
  - angles at a point on a straight line and half a turn (total 180°)
  - other multiples of 90°
- use the properties of rectangles to deduce related facts and find missing lengths and angles
- distinguish between regular and irregular polygons based on reasoning about equal sides and angles

This means that we should spend at least one week teaching children about angles so that they can master these elements, particularly the drawing and measuring of angles.

In Year 6, children should be using what they have mastered in Year 5 to find unknown angles in any triangles, quadrilaterals and regular polygons and to recognise angles where they meet at a point, are on a straight line or are vertically opposite. This is quite a tall order if the children have not achieved the Year 5 requirements.

Encouraging children to estimate angles based on their understanding of acute, obtuse and reflex angles, before measuring and to compare their actual measurements with their estimates, is important.

Introducing the concept of angles to the children through art is a really nice idea.

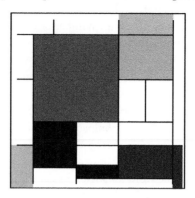

I have used Piet Mondrian's painting, *Composition no. 8*, as a starting point for various lessons in Years 3 and 4. One lesson was shape and angles. The painting clearly demonstrates squares and oblongs, parallel and perpendicular sides and right angles. We talk about what we notice, things that are the same and things that are different. Then I give them pieces of different-coloured paper, and their task is to draw around square and oblong faces of 3D shapes and create their own version of a Mondrian.

Another starting point is for fractions. You can clearly see in the painting that some rectangles are fractions of others, so we identify those we can see. The children then cut out the pieces and start exploring the pieces to see what fractions they can find. The results have been amazing! One child said to me, 'This first piece is one third of the second piece and this third piece is half of this first one, so it must be one sixth of the second.' Once they have explored, they then make a pattern with one line of symmetry using the cut-out pieces. These made a great display.

Wassily Kandinsky's *Composition with Large Red Plane, Yellow, Black, Grey and Blue* (1921) is brilliant for quadrilaterals, circles and acute, obtuse and reflex angles. I use this as a starting point for angles. We have lots of discussion about what we can see. We discuss concentric circles, curved and straight lines, as well as the obvious quadrilaterals and angles. The task I give them is to draw acute and obtuse angles on a piece of plain paper. They then decorate it by drawing and colouring different quadrilaterals. Again, this makes an attractive display.

When linking mathematics and art in this way, beginning with a potted history of the artist and showing examples of their work are important.

In the archives of the National Centre for Excellence in Teaching Mathematics' *Primary Magazine* are many issues that focus on mathematics and art. You will find information on many artists, examples of their work and mathematical ideas for each painting.

I often give Year 5 children activities similar to the one that follows.

The idea of this is that the children work with a partner. They take it in turns to pick a card showing an angle. They estimate the size of the angle first and write their estimate in a table. They then measure it and find the difference between the actual measurement and their estimate. The child who scores the least number of points is the winner.

Cards include the following.

Diagram 5.9

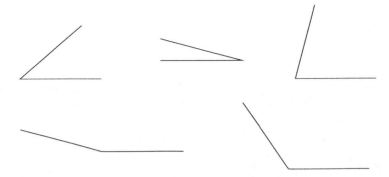

The table the children complete looks something like this:

Type (acute or obtuse)	Estimate	Actual	Difference

Another activity I like to work on with Year 6 children is to explore angles in regular and irregular polygons. They know by now that a triangle has a total internal angle size of 180°. I ask them to use this information to show the total internal angles of a quadrilateral, a pentagon and a hexagon and then to make up a generalisation that works for finding the total angles of any polygon.

Diagram 5.10

The following are examples.

You can see from the preceding diagrams that the polygons can be divided into triangles when drawing diagonals from corner or vertex to corner or vertex.

One triangle = 180°
One square = two triangles = 180° × 2 = 360°
One pentagon = three triangles = 180° × 3 = 540°
One hexagon = four triangles = 180° × 4 = 720°

Note that the number of triangles that the shape can be divided into is always two fewer than the sides of the shape.

If *n* represents the number of sides a shape has, then the generalisation would be 180° × (*n* − 2).

The NNS produced a useful Interactive Teaching Programme called 'Calculating Angles', a tool to use when modelling how to use a protractor. This is still available, although a search on the internet is likely to produce other similar tools.

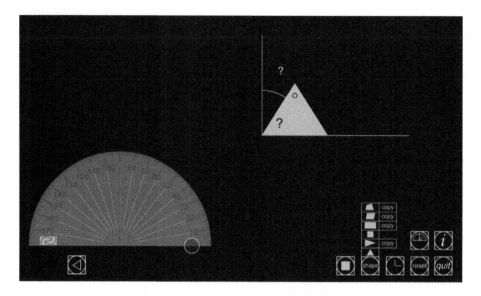

Position and direction

Year 1 are expected to describe position, direction and movement. There are no descriptive words in the requirements, but there are suggested words in the notes and guidance. These are *left and right; top, middle and bottom; on top of, in front of, above; between, around; near, close and far; up and down; forwards and backwards;* and *inside and outside*. Relating these to the 3D shapes children are working with is a good idea. You could ask them to position, for example, a cube to the right of the table and underneath a chair, a sphere to the left of the cube and a cylinder on top of the chair.

Year 1 also need to make whole, half, quarter and three-quarter turns. There is an obvious link to fractions here, so you could ask children to make these turns to the right or left when working on halves and quarters in fractions.

Year 2 are expected to use mathematical vocabulary to describe position, direction and movement. Again, no specific vocabulary is in the requirements, and there is none in the notes and guidance. It probably would be a good idea to rehearse the vocabulary suggested for Year 1.

Children extend the Year 1 curriculum for quarter, half and three-quarter turns, this time referring to turns in a clockwise and anti-clockwise direction. Again, linking these to work on fractions would be sensible. They begin to explore movement in a straight line, which is the first steps towards translations.

A translation is simply a movement in a straight direction, forwards or backwards. We make translations all the time, for example, when we walk in a straight line from one place to another; a football makes a translation when it is kicked in a straight line. Translations are very common, and we should use the correct word when referring to this concept.

They begin to simply explore rotations as a turn and in terms of right angles. A rotation is a movement that has a central point that stays fixed and everything else moves around that point in a circle. When working on rotation, the children need to do this practically.

If you have programmable robots, giving the children opportunities to programme these to move in straight lines and to make clockwise and anti-clockwise rotations is a good idea.

In Key Stage 2, revisiting and consolidating work carried out in Year 2 to keep these concepts fresh is a good idea.

Coordinates

Children are first introduced to coordinates in Year 4, so this will be new learning for them. It is important that enough time is spent on this area so that the children master what they need to learn in order to build upon their understanding in Years 5 and 6. The work done at a primary level lays the foundations for further algebraic work in secondary school when children study, for example, Cartesian graphs.

A coordinate grid or coordinate plane is basically a 2D number line. The horizontal line is called the x-axis, and the vertical line is called the y-axis. These two lines are perpendicular, and they cross at their zero points. This point is called the origin.

The axes divide the grid or plane into four parts; each part is called a quadrant. Quadrant 1 is the top-right quadrant, and the numbers found here are all positive. Quadrant 2 is the top-left quadrant; the numbers on the y-axis are positive, and those on the x-axis numbers are negative. Quadrant 3 is the bottom-left quadrant, and all the numbers here are negative. The final quadrant is quadrant 4; the numbers on the x-axis are positive, and those on the y-axis are negative. When reading coordinates, the number from the x-axis is read first, followed by the number on the y-axis. The two coordinates are always bracketed together and separated by a comma, for example, (2,5), (2,7), (4,5) and (4,7). These coordinates would make a two-by-two square.

In Year 4, children are expected to describe positions on a 2D grid as coordinates in the first quadrant. In Year 6, children explore the complete four-quadrant coordinate grid or plane. The requirements for Year 5 do not mention coordinates, but as the notes and guidance suggest, they still need to work on coordinates in the first quadrant for activities using reflections and translations. These suggestions reflect the Year 5 requirement to identify, describe and represent the position of a shape following a reflection or translation, using the appropriate language, and know that the shape has not changed. The notes and guidance add that this should be carried out on a coordinate plane in the first quadrant. Building this up and including the second quadrant so that the children can reflect across the y-axis might be a good idea.

The following diagram is of a complete coordinate plane. Geography is an obvious link to coordinates. To practise this, you might give the children opportunities to identify locations on a map by giving the grid references, which are basically coordinates.

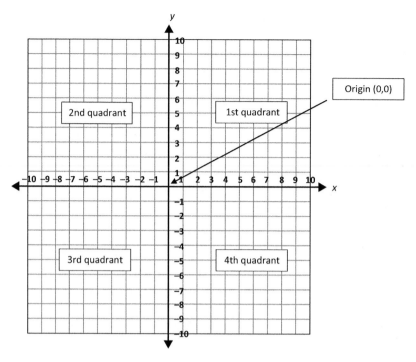

Year 6 are required to describe positions on the coordinate plane shown above. They are also required to draw and translate simple shapes onto it and to reflect them across the axes.

To be competent to do this, children, obviously, need to have mastered the Year 4 curriculum requirements, which are to describe positions on a 2D grid as coordinates in the first quadrant, to describe movements between position as translations of a given unit to the left/right and up/down and, finally, to plot specified points and draw sides to complete a given polygon.

Following is the type of grid, Years 4 and 5 children should have access to.

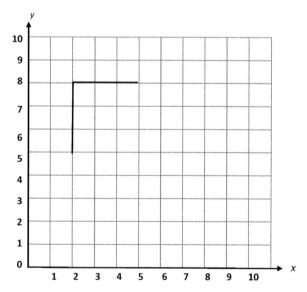

Activities could include asking the children to plot different coordinates, x-axis first and then the y-axis. They should put a small cross where the coordinates on two axes meet. After they are confident doing this, they plot their own coordinates and record them. Then you could give them two coordinates; ask them to make an equilateral, isosceles or scalene triangle; and record the missing coordinate. Repeat this for quadrilaterals, for example, in the earlier grid, give the children the coordinates (2,8), (5,8) and (2,5), the children then work out the other coordinate to complete the square. This coordinate would be (5,5). You could give the same three coordinates and ask them to complete a trapezium, which could be (6,5), (7,5) or other x-axis points to go with the 5 on the y-axis. They could then make a kite with the extra coordinate at, for example, (7,3). Keeping the initial three coordinates the same and varying the others is a good example of variation. Then move onto other shapes, such as irregular pentagons and hexagons.

You could extend the work in Year 5 so that children work on the first two quadrants. They could then reflect and translate across the y-axis.

The main messages from this section are to ensure that we use the correct vocabulary for the shapes that we are teaching and that we ensure that we teach shape in depth, adjusting the national curriculum as we need to so that, for example, 3D shapes are covered in every year and coordinates are revisited in Year 5.

References

Derek, H, *Mathematics explained for primary teachers*, 4th edn, Sage Publications, Thousand Oaks, CA, 2010.

Maths is Fun, https://www.mathsisfun.com

National Curriculum, 2014, gov,uk

Nrich, https://nrich.maths.org/.

Index